The Investigative State: Regulatory Oversight in the United States

Daniel Zachary Epstein

The Investigative State: Regulatory Oversight in the United States

palgrave
macmillan

Daniel Zachary Epstein
Law
St. Thomas University
Miami, FL, USA

ISBN 978-3-031-38460-8 ISBN 978-3-031-38461-5 (eBook)
https://doi.org/10.1007/978-3-031-38461-5

This Palgrave Macmillan imprint is published by the registered company Springer Nature Switzerland AG
The registered company address is: Gewerbestrasse 11, 6330 Cham, Switzerland

Preface

The federal bureaucracy exists today because Congress delegated its policymaking responsibility to create executive branch agencies. “Oversight” ensures that delegated legislative power remains accountable and responsive to the people, most directly through Congress. American politics and administrative law are related in their joint examination of congressional delegation and oversight by Congress and the courts. Scholars interested in the intersection of delegation and oversight have long debated whether oversight of the bureaucracy is effective. The research question commonly posed is whether Congress has the “capacity” for oversight—the extent to which Congress has the available resources (in terms of committee budgets and staffing as well as the volume of hearings) to effectively oversee the bureaucracy. This book is ultimately skeptical that spending taxpayer dollars on more congressional staff or other committee resources will move the needle in restraining bureaucratic drift from legislative preferences. This book instead sides with those scholars who find that new institutional arrangements and statutory procedures can curb bureaucratic drift even if Congress does not appear to be aggressively flexing its oversight muscle popularly conceived: through aggressive, expertly prepared public hearings.

The contribution of “The Investigative State” fits within the positive political theory literature which theorizes that Congress can effectuate its oversight goals through legal procedures. My primary contribution to the literature is that not so unlike how Congress relies on delegation to advance policy goals in the form of regulation, Congress also relies on delegation to advance its policy goals in the form of oversight. I show that in authorizing agencies with subpoena powers and creating Inspectors General—executive branch officials tasked with overseeing agency expenditures and programs, and the employees who implement them—Congress has delegated the hard work of monitoring the bureaucracy to more permanent experts. My contention is that Congress's preferred mode of oversight is to delegate the oversight power itself. My empirical work further supports the argument that Congress strategically develops administrative procedures to promote the ability of members to use oversight to advance their electoral interests. This conclusion has implications for political theories on the Constitution and the separation of powers, for if administrative procedures are inherently political, then the judiciary should be cautious in reviewing such procedures.

Validating the model of delegated oversight requires reexamining several assumptions within the American politics literature. While the goal of oversight might be subject to substantial consensus among scholars, the nature of the oversight power is not. The concept of congressional oversight within the political science literature does not include investigations of non-bureaucratic targets as part of oversight—for instance, congressional investigations of the President or of businesses are excluded from the received concept of oversight. In practice, this means that government watchdog groups are included within the scope of "oversight" whereas bureaucratic investigations of businesses are not. Yet both originate from Congress's constitutional power of inquiry. Moreover, because scholars relate oversight to delegation, the assumption is that the need for "oversight" did not arise prior to the creation of the modern regulatory state. This assumption rests on a narrow idea of legislative policymaking and its delegation. Scholars tend to examine legislative power as limited to legislation that establishes rules binding the public and the bureaucracy as exercising such legislative power through rulemaking. But a historical examination of legislative power and its delegation reveals a broad understanding of legislative power to include not merely the power to write rules but to conduct investigations of the private sphere in order to craft those rules.

Furthermore, prior to Congress delegating its rulemaking powers to agencies, it delegated its investigative powers, exercising bureaucratic oversight by retaining its power to craft rules of law. Thus, our federal regulatory state began as an investigative state. And as the regulatory state evolved through increasing congressional delegation, so too did the nature of oversight. The book's empirical work presents an empirical model of the theoretical insight that Congress relies on administrative procedures in the law to constrain bureaucratic policymaking.

Given the congressional oversight activities toward the Trump administration, it should not be surprising that Congress strategically delegates its oversight power to achieve its public policy goals. The first impeachment of President Trump resulted from findings released to Congress from the Intelligence Community Inspector General. Congress was able to effectuate its interests in accessing the former president's financial information as well as obtain White House records through procedures that allow congressional committees to force compliance with its subpoenas in court. Indeed, the January 6 Committee relied on tools permitting it to investigate *former* government officials and private citizens—not a contemporaneous federal bureaucracy.

This book's historical analysis and empirical results present strong implications for constitutional and administrative law. Debate among legal scholars and practitioners before the Supreme Court on the nondelegation doctrine, which states Congress cannot empower the executive branch to exercise legislative power unless policymaking standards guide such authorizations, must now confront the book's empirical findings showing that Congress delegates legislative power unrelated to policymaking goals to reduce its workload and maximize electoral benefits to its members. Relatedly, if the purpose of oversight is primarily electoral, this should inform whether interbranch oversight disputes are appropriate for judicial review. And the legislative procedure wherein congressional investigations are incidental to legislation ought to apply as a constraint over investigations by corporate watchdogs like the SEC and FTC as necessary to rulemaking as opposed to a status quo where these investigations are seen as adjuncts to civil or criminal penalties.

Beyond these implications for legal doctrine, the book also pushes our theoretical understanding of the federal bureaucracy. That Congress conducts oversight through laws that empower Inspectors General or arm citizens with the ability to go to court to challenge agency policymaking reflects that power in the regulatory state rests not with the president or the appointees who run executive branch agencies, but in individuals and organized interests who set the administrative law agenda before Congress and the courts. Rather than the American federal bureaucracy being a centralized state unified by presidential power, it is a pluralistic one. That American bureaucratic power is pluralistic distinguishes the American federal bureaucracy from other contemporaneous or historical examples throughout the globe. And it highlights the ways in which the modern administrative state must be theorized in democratic terms.

Miami, USA

Daniel Zachary Epstein

Contents

List of Figures

Chapter 2

Chapter 4

List of Tables

Chapter 4

CHAPTER 1

Introduction

Of all the concepts studied by observers of American politics, congressional oversight may be the one most recognized within the public imagination. Neither academics nor casual political observers dispute that congressional oversight is a "good" thing. Scholars of congressional oversight readily acknowledge that oversight is a tool with which Congress checks the executive branch and one which is most readily observed through committee hearings. The challenge for political science has been how to explain variation in congressional oversight activity and how to assess its efficacy. Scholars may agree that oversight serves as a constitutional check by controlling the implementation of bureaucratic policy but disagree as to whether Congress succeeds in that endeavor. And scholars may further disagree whether members engage in oversight for ideological or partisan reasons. Lastly, how scholars conceptualize oversight—for instance, does Congress prefer to conduct oversight through hard-charging investigative hearings or through other, less frequent, means?—leads to differing inferences about whether congressional capacity for oversight is increasing or declining over time.

The literature often presents the above explanations for oversight as competing alternatives, where one explanation is mutually exclusive of the alternative explanation. The literature does not address the possibility of a more complex picture, where Congress might rely on oversight via both administrative procedures and hearings to advance different

D. Z. Epstein, *The Investigative State: Regulatory Oversight in the United States*, https://doi.org/10.1007/978-3-031-38461-5_1

interests, whether ideological or electoral. This book contributes to the political science literature by providing a fuller account of the tools for examining oversight, understanding its breadth as well as its ramifications. The title of this book, "The Investigative State," is informed by the origin story of the federal bureaucracy. The federal regulatory state began when Congress delegated to the executive branch its investigative powers, rather than the power to write regulations, retaining its power to enact rules as law as its original oversight role. Delineating this history between congressional delegation and oversight of the bureaucracy is crucial to unpacking the scope of legislative power and its delegation, a symbiotic nexus underlying a full account of congressional oversight.

The book is organized into two theoretical chapters and a main empirical chapter. Rather than provide an overview of those chapters here, I will instead outline what I view as the six major research themes of the project. First, the concept of congressional oversight within the political science literature does not account for oversight activities targeted beyond the bureaucracy or bureaucratic activities external to policymaking. Second, this underinclusive concept of oversight results from a narrow understanding of legislative power and, therefore, the scope of what can be delegated by Congress. Third, updating the ways in which political scientists understand legislative power and delegation informs the academic understanding of oversight. Fourth, and illustrating the prior observation, rather than choosing between police patrols and fire alarms, Congress uses administrative procedures to create fire chiefs—the Inspectors General—within the bureaucracy who monitor policy, i.e., engage in oversight. Fifth, the congressional choice to delegate its oversight power by creating Inspectors General allows congressional members to more effectively use congressional oversight hearings to achieve their electoral interests. Sixth, the picture that emerges from the theoretical and empirical contributions of this book has normative implications for administrative and constitutional law: because members benefit electorally when administrative procedures are attached to policy-agnostic statutes rather than when procedures are contained in laws specific to agency policymaking, the legal distinction between law enforcement and legislative agencies has strong validity and the use of congressional oversight to advance members' electoral interests means interbranch information disputes are not appropriate for judicial review.

1 The Underinclusive Concept of Oversight

The concept of oversight among political scientists results from a descriptive account of the need for elected officials to monitor bureaucratic implementation of policy established in legislation.[1] Bureaucratic policymaking is typically observed as a form of regulation called rules.[2] For political scientists, delegation occurs when Congress legislatively empowers agencies to administer policies with the force of law. Delegation is of scholarly interest because of the expectation that elected officials will be motivated to ensure agencies exercising delegated authority do so in a way consistent with political preferences. An obvious, yet subtle, point is that oversight and delegation are interrelated.

Political scientists identify oversight as focused on the bureaucracy and that often translates to "independent agencies" or the congressionally mandated (in legal terms, "ministerial" as opposed to "discretionary") responsibilities assigned to executive officers overseeing statutorily directed programs. But the scholarship does not articulate a model for investigative activities aimed at targets other than the bureaucracy, for example, House Intelligence Committee investigations into the president's foreign diplomatic activities or a Senate Permanent Subcommittee on Investigations subpoena to an Internet company accused of exploiting children. Are those activities "oversight"? Because the current model of oversight is concerned with monitoring the implementation of public policy by unelected officials, congressional investigations of the president (and his copartisans in the executive branch) or the private sphere are not included within the received concept of oversight. Similarly, to the extent definitions of oversight are limited to the monitoring of policy, then Inspectors General would not fit within this received model either. This presents an explanatory difficulty, for in political practice, rhetoric by the media, special interests, and legislators is often employed to demand that the president or the private sphere be held accountable—by none other than congressional "oversight."

[1] David Epstein & Sharyn O'Halloran, *Administrative Procedures Information, and Agency Discretion*, J. L. Econ. & Org. (1994) at 701.

[2] *Id.* at 702.

2 Broadening the Conception of Legislative Power

Congress's public policy powers include not only writing standards into rules of law but also fact-gathering investigations of the private sphere in order to inform those rules. Further, central to Congress's authority is its impeachment power which has always justified investigations focused on the president and his administration. If Congress writes rules, investigates the private sphere, and investigates political officials, then Congress has the choice to delegate any or all of these powers to the bureaucracy. And if oversight concerns monitoring bureaucratic compliance with legislative goals, then a theory of oversight must be able to account for delegation of legislative powers beyond rules of conduct that bind the public.

3 The Punctuated Nature of Congressional Delegation and the Investigative State

Congressional delegation—both in terms of what powers are authorized and who is tasked with their exercise—is punctuated by legal and political change. In Congress's first 100 years, it delegated its powers to committees, courts, the president and Cabinet officials before the first agency was created. Congress also, from its beginning, assigned legislative responsibilities to executive officers—ranging from establishing laws to govern territorial governments to rules governing the issuance of patents.[3] This assignment of "ministerial duties" to the president and executive officers is distinct, in time and substance, from the assignment of legislative responsibilities to an entire department or agency. When the federal bureaucracy is formally created in 1887, Congress does not vest it with rulemaking powers but investigative ones. Unlike examples of centralized regulatory agencies throughout western Europe, the American federal regulatory state decidedly begins as an investigative state. Not until the twentieth century does Congress empower the bureaucracy with the power to enact rules with the force of law.

[3] Mortenson & Bagley, 121 Colum. L. Rev. at 336–337 note 245, *supra*. *See also* Jerry L. Mashaw, *Reluctant Nationalists: Federal Administration and Administrative Law in the Republican Era, 1801–1829*, 116 Yale L.J. 1636, 1708 (2007) (discussing rules binding regulatory conduct versus rules with the force of law binding the private sector).

The administrative state therefore arises from the congressional choice to delegate the legislative power to investigate to an entire office (i.e., an agency), not simply to a single officer. The political development of the modern American bureaucracy has been shaped by different forms of delegation at different times. Congressional delegation is chronologically disrupted, or punctuated, by the changing identity of the congressional agent empowered with legislative responsibilities: committees, then courts, then executive officers, then agencies.

At the Founding, Congress delegated both its investigative and adjudicatory powers over the private sphere to committees for the purpose of passing private bills. Throughout the nineteenth century, Congress assigned adjudicatory and investigative powers to executive branch officers. Beginning in the late nineteenth century, Congress began delegating those investigative and adjudicatory powers beyond just executive branch officers but to agencies located within the executive branch and overseen by executive officers while assigning rulemaking responsibilities to principal executive branch officers.[4] At this time, Congress retained the power to make rules.[5] Only in the early twentieth century did Congress

[4] Jerry L. Mashaw, *Federal Administration and Administrative Law in the Gilded Age*, 119 Yale L.J. 1362, 1398 (2010).

[5] In addition to Mashaw, Nicholas Parrillo argues that Congress delegated rulemaking to executive officers early in the Republic. *See* Nicholas R. Parrillo, *A Critical Assessment of the Originalist Case Against Administrative Regulatory Power: New Evidence from the Federal Tax on Private Real Estate in the 1790s*, 130 Yale L.J. 1288–1651 (2021). Parrillo argued that Congress in 1798 authorized federal commissioners to conduct "[i]ntrastate mass tax valuation revisions" which the Supreme Court determined to be rulemaking in *Bi-Metallic Investment Co. v. State Board of Equalization* (1915). However, three reasons distinguish Parrillo's findings from being considered the sort of delegation of legislative power over the entire nation scholars focus on when they discuss rulemaking. First, the commissioners appointed through the Valuation and Enumeration Act of 1798, 1 Stat. 580 (Chapter 70) were not "tax commissioners." They were assessors; the act of collecting revenue was performed by separate officers enumerated in 1 Stat. 591, Section 6 (Chapter 71) ("Collectors of the Revenue"). Second, *Bi-Metallic Inv. Co. v. State Bd. of Equalization* did not involve the question of congressional delegation of rulemaking but whether the 14th Amendment's due process guarantees applied to state rulemaking. The rule in question in *Bi-Metallic Inv. Co.* was an "order of the boards increasing the valuation of all taxable property in Denver forty per cent." 239 U.S. 441, 443 (1915). The 1798 V&E Act established no power in the commissioners to establish a tax rate nor enforce that rate. Instead, they were granted discretion to modify assessed property values for a given district but that didn't change the fact that the tax formula (progressive tax up to 1% of dwelling houses valued above $100, $.50 tax per slave, and a fixed rate tax of real property) was carried out by the collectors of revenue, not the commissioners.

first delegate to an agency its rulemaking power over the private sphere, what is commonly thought to be the power to legislate.[6] "Oversight" originates as a concept only once Congress delegates this rulemaking power.

These punctuations in delegation both informed, and were informed by, law. The transition from Congress's delegation of powers to committees to the delegation of powers to executive branch officers through statute was made possible by early Supreme Court doctrine that referred to such statutes not as delegations but as assignments of "ministerial" responsibilities to executive branch officers. The idea that Congress could

Third, there is no question that the commissioners were engaged in adjudication, not rulemaking. Section 20 of the V&E Act explains the appellate process for challenging the assessment of one's property by the district assessors. The standard for adjudicating those challenges was "just and equitable." Under Section 21, the principal assessors then submitted their final determinations to the commissioners who, pursuant to Section 22 and when acting as a state majority, could further adjust the district assessment value. The fact that Section 22 authorizes the commissioners to deduct or enhance assessment values but cannot "change[]" or "affect[]" the relative valuations of other property by definition means that the commissioners' revision authority concerned individual property values not the total value assessed for a district. We see this principle more clearly stated in Section 23 which allows the commissioners to order the assessors "to add to, or deduct from the valuations of the lands and dwelling-houses of each individual, such a rate per centum, as shall be determined by the commissioners, as aforesaid." Finally, every abstract of the property in the district was presented to the commission after an opportunity for adjudication. When reviewing the abstract presented, the commissioners had equitable powers because Section 22 made them personally liable to the Treasury Department in failing to confirm whether certain property was exempted from taxation under state law (Section 25), whether a slave who was not actively working was improperly assessed, or whether property was transferred or built yet improperly valued.

[6] Jerry Mashaw references the Steamboat Safety Act of 1852 as authorizing rulemaking by an agency. *See* Jerry L. Mashaw, ***Administration and "The Democracy": Administrative Law from Jackson to Lincoln, 1829–1861***, 117 Yale L.J. 1568, 1640 (2008). The rulemaking authority of the 9 presidentially appointed supervising inspectors, acting collectively, concerned only rules applying to the supervising inspectors and local boards of inspectors. *See* Act of Aug. 30, 1852, ch. 106, § 18, 10 Stat. 61, 70. Under Section 29 of the Act, "it shall be the duty of the supervising inspectors to establish such rules and regulations to be observed by all such vessels in passing each other[.]" *Id.* at § 29. These rules, however, were not enacted through the 9 appointed supervising inspectors acting jointly but were instead established by each supervising inspector independently. As Mashaw acknowledges, "[t]he contributions of the Jacksonian era to modern administrative law are thus to be found largely in the understandings that are reflected in the perennial competition between congresses and presidents for political control of administration, and in the internal rules, practices, and systems of the administrative agencies and departments themselves." Mashaw, 117 Yale L.J. at 1688.

statutorily encumber presidents and the Cabinet is crucial to the political validity of oversight and the result of the Supreme Court's determination that certain executive branch officials must act "under the authority of law, and not by the instructions of the president."[7] A "ministerial act" is one "which the law enjoins on a particular officer for a particular purpose."[8] Oversight depends upon the idea that in carrying out statutorily required ("ministerial") acts, executive branch officials are accountable to Congress, not the president.

The 1838 Supreme Court reaffirmed this principle in *Kendall v. United States ex rel. Stokes*.[9] In *Kendall*, the question presented was whether the federal judiciary could enforce a law to require an executive officer appointed by the president to perform a statutory duty.[10] The Supreme Court answered the question in the affirmative, distinguishing between an executive officer's "discharge of any official duty, partaking in any respect of an executive character" and "the performance of a mere ministerial act, which neither he nor the president had any authority to deny or control."[11] The principle that Congress could assign responsibilities to political officials selected by the president, combined with the conclusion that the president lacked authority over the performance of such duties, formed a legal foundation for congressional inquiries into how a presidential administration was carrying out legislative goals. Moreover, the *Kendall* Court eviscerated the notion of the "unitary executive" where the president exclusively directs and controls those executive officers subject to his appointment.[12] The *Kendall* decision also complicates

[7] *Marbury v. Madison*, 5 U.S. (1 Cranch) 137, 158 (1803).

[8] *Id.*

[9] *See* Daniel Epstein, *Kendall v. United States and the Inspector General Dilemma*, Univ. of Chicago L. Rev. Online (June 2020), https://lawreviewblog.uchicago.edu/2020/06/22/ig-dilemma-epstein/.

[10] *Kendall v. United States*, 37 U.S. 524, 611 (1838).

[11] *Id.* at 610.

[12] *Id. Compare to Myers v. United States*, 272 U.S. 52, 135 (1926) ("[t]he ordinary duties of officers prescribed by statute come under the general administrative control of the president by virtue of the general grant to him of the executive power, and he may properly supervise and guide their construction of the statutes under which they act in order to secure that unitary and uniform execution of the laws which Article II of the Constitution evidently contemplated in vesting general executive power in the president alone. Laws are often passed with specific provision for the adoption of regulations by a department or bureau head to make the law workable and effective. The ability and

the assumption that Congress simply wrote laws that the president (and his appointees) enforced. Congress could now direct executive officers to sign judicial commissions or award money to claimants and these officials have no discretion to refrain from doing what Congress instructs. These "ministerial"—as opposed to constitutional—duties were those where Congress had "superior authority" over the president "to command" official acts.[13]

The *Kendall* Court took care to lay out principles of administrative law by instructing that an executive officer's failure to carry out a statutory duty was tantamount to seeking to "control congress" because the officer lacked any discretion over a "matter resting entirely in the discretion of congress."[14] By distinguishing between the president's constitutional responsibilities and the ministerial responsibilities Congress mandates upon the executive branch, the Supreme Court established that Congress may place obligations upon executive officers and affected parties may obtain a legal remedy to noncompliance. Congress's constitutional sanction to assign ministerial obligations onto law enforcement officers made possible the ability to assign obligations to an entire department of the executive branch. Constitutional scholars characterize oversight in terms of "congressional oversight of administration"[15] and political scientists similarly describe oversight as "[c]ongressional control of the bureaucracy."[16] In practice, and as informed by the jurisprudence antecedent

judgment manifested by the official thus empowered, as well as his energy and stimulation of his subordinates, are subjects which the president must consider and supervise in his administrative control").

[13] Kendall, 37 U.S., *supra* note 10 at 611; *accord*. Webster's Dictionary (1838), *available at* http://www.webstersdictionary1828.com/Dictionary/ministerial.

[14] Kendall, note 10 at 611. The Court described the notion that a presidentially appointed officer could resist a ministerial duty the equivalent of vesting the president with "a dispensing power" and "would be clothing the president with a power entirely to control the legislation of congress, and paralyze the administration of justice." *Id.* at 613.

[15] Gillian E. Metzger, *The Constitutional Duty to Supervise*, 124 Yale L.J. 1836, 1930 (2015); *accord*. Arthur W. MacMahon, *Congressional Oversight of Administration: The Power of the Purse I*, 68 Pol. Sci. Q. 161 (1943); Arthur W. MacMahon, *Congressional Oversight of Administration: The Power of the Purse II*, 68 Pol. Sci. Q. 380 (1943).

[16] David Epstein & Sharyn O'Halloran, *A Theory of Strategic Oversight: Congress, Lobbyists, and the Bureaucracy*, 11 J. L. Econ. & Org. (1995) at 227.

to the creation of the bureaucracy, oversight implies that there are non-discretionary requirements of executive branch officers and employees which are subject to congressional supervision and control.

Once the Interstate Commerce Commission is established in 1887, the Supreme Court took caution to emphasize that Congress's assigning ministerial powers to an executive officer is simply authorization to enforce the law, not delegation.[17] Because the nineteenth-century administrative state was an "investigative state" the Supreme Court also held that congressional assignment of its investigative powers to an agency while retaining authority over "regulation" is not delegation.[18] The legislative power, then, is conceived as the authority to make law separate from its enforcement. As such, the administrative subpoenas which characterized the activity of the incipient bureaucracy, "are not to be construed as authorizing enforcement."[19]

In response to continuing public pressure concerning the increasing power of railroads, their holding companies, and the impact on industrial workers, Congress, most prominently from 1903 to 1910, delegated its rulemaking powers. Up until this time, the regulation of industry was carried out by congressional investigations from 1789 to 1887 and executive branch investigations from 1887 to 1902. The federal regulatory state that emerged in the early twentieth century was preceded by a federal investigative state. That Congress's decision to delegate its investigative powers and its power to write rules was punctuated by legal and political developments is crucial to understanding that delegation is conditioned by Congress's evolving need to maximize electoral returns on its direct activities while minimizing resource-intensive costs of minimal electoral value. Not only do scholars generally overlook the administrative state's investigative versus rulemaking origins, scholars and jurists identify Congress's original decision to delegate as coextensive with the creation of the federal regulatory state. Rather than delegation being fixed in time, its punctuated nature reflects a legislative strategy to accommodate the electoral needs of members when public expectations dictate institutional change.

[17] *Marshall Field & Co. v. Clark*, 143 U.S. 649, 693 (1892).

[18] *Interstate Commerce Comm'n v. Goodrich Transit Co.*, 224 U.S. 194, 211 (1912).

[19] *Oklahoma Press Pub. Co. v. Walling*, 327 U.S. 186, 201 (1946).

4 Delegating Oversight: Fire Chiefs and Oversight Efficiency

Oversight is causally connected to the delegation of legislative power. Because congressional delegation, as a historical and constitutional matter, is broader than the assignment of legislative policymaking to the limited set of bureaucratic rulemaking, the scope of oversight must likewise be broader than the mere monitoring of agency rules. Instead, congressional "oversight" extends to monitoring delegation to the bureaucracy of rulemaking, private sector investigating, and investigations of judicial and executive officers.

In this broad formulation, congressional oversight targets the president, the bureaucracy, and the private sphere, for it is the right to monitor how legislative agents exercise delegated power. The administrative state acts with all of the legislative powers identified by the earlier historical summary: it conducts investigations of the private sphere, issues legislative rules and orders with the force of law that bind private parties, and it investigates political officials' compliance with statutory responsibilities ("ministerial duties"). If it is delegated, it can be overseen. This formulation accords with popular sentiment and political rhetoric on congressional oversight. For instance, oversight is said to vindicate the taxpayers' (and legislative appropriators') right to know how their money is being spent.[20]

But a central puzzle the academic study of congressional oversight must confront is why Congress still dedicates any of its oversight resources to standing committees if Congress prefers to conduct oversight by enacting administrative procedures into law. Scholars have intimated that committees must matter even in the presence of self-executing administrative procedures because the information about agency infractions that result from constituent complaints (fire alarms) must nevertheless be transmitted to Congress or otherwise inform its public oversight agenda. While scholars have examined the effects of rulemaking delegation on oversight, no scholar has methodically examined the effects of Congress's

[20] "[A] democracy cannot function unless the people are permitted to know what their government is up to." *United States DOJ v. Reporters Comm. for Freedom of Press*, 489 U.S. 749, 772–773 (1989) (quoting EPA v. Mink, 410 U.S. 73, 105 (1973)) (quoting Henry Steele Commager, N.Y. Rev. of Books (Oct. 5, 1972) at 7).

delegating its other powers—investigations over the private sphere and political officials—on Congress's public agenda, viz., oversight hearings.

The empirical contribution of this book examines the original delegation to the bureaucracy in the form of statutes authorizing agencies with subpoena powers over private businesses and individuals ("administrative subpoenas"). Because congressional delegation is punctuated by the constant need to accommodate members' electoral preferences with public expectations, I also examine a more recent form of delegation: the establishment of Inspectors General (IGs)—bureaucratic monitors ("fire chiefs") housed within the bureaucracy. The significance of this empirical strategy is not simply a test of the relationship between delegation and oversight. Independent of whether the concept of oversight captures *prima facie* congressional investigations of political officials or only those investigations responding to how these officials exercise ministerial obligations, the concept of oversight certainly includes the case where the power of inquiry over officials is delegated to the bureaucracy. Thus, the study of IGs presents the opportunity to examine the phenomenon of Congress choosing to delegate the legislative power of oversight. The possibility that Congress can delegate a power itself contingent on the act of delegation further illustrates the causal relationship between oversight and delegation as well as the punctuated nature of delegation as legislative needs evolve over time.

I present these expectations about delegation in the context of my strategy for identifying congressional oversight hearings. My analysis of oversight shows that, as a general matter, Congress is engaging in more oversight hearings over time, with less time being spent per hearing. I describe this trend as reflecting a preference for "oversight efficiency." My interest is determining whether delegation has causal effects on oversight efficiency. To examine that possibility, I develop an original data set of all administrative subpoena authorities created by Congress from 1912 to the present. If administrative subpoenas are, as the Supreme Court has stated, a "delegated power" and an "adjunct to the power of legislation" and congressional oversight is *ex post* delegation, then I expect that administrative subpoena authorizations should influence congressional oversight and oversight efficiency in particular. Otherwise, I would lack the evidence to reject the alternative hypothesis that administrative subpoena authorizations are simply expansions of executive branch law enforcement powers. By using an instrumental variable model that correlates the effects of administrative subpoena authorizations on congressional oversight as mediated through administrative rulemaking, I can make causal inferences about whether Congress, in delegating agency subpoena powers, retains control over its own investigative powers.

My results show no statistical support for the effects of administrative subpoena authorizations on congressional oversight. If oversight measures congressional control over delegated power, then either Congress fails to control its delegation of investigative authority to the bureaucracy or Congress exercises control over agency investigations in another manner. An additional possibility is that given the language of administrative subpoena procedures has been unchanged over their near 150-year history, congressional choices about specifying such procedures within particular policy schemes versus as executive branch-wide requirements, in addition to changing legal institutions, electoral dynamics or political norms, may have shifted the meaning and significance of these laws.

Because I am also interested in the extent to which Congress delegates its oversight powers, I develop an original causal model examining the effects of the passage of the Inspector General Act on congressional oversight activities. My examination of the IG Act is also a strategy for making inferences about how Congress prefers to monitor its delegated authority. The IG Act empowers Inspectors General to issue administrative subpoenas over individuals and companies in order to police compliance with federal contracting laws. In fact, most administrative subpoena activity from the bureaucracy each year comes from the Inspectors General acting in this role. But the IG Act also grants IGs investigative powers over executive agency employees and programs with the caveat that IGs cannot use administrative subpoenas against the government.

By examining IGs, the model allows me to distinguish the effects on congressional oversight resulting from investigations of the private sphere versus investigations of the bureaucracy. It also allows for inferences to be made about how Congress chooses to delegate a given power. The administrative subpoena authority granted to the Inspectors General is the standard language that can be found in hundreds of statutes authorizing Cabinet secretaries, commissioners, or administrative law judges to issue administrative subpoenas. The difference between these latter statutes and the IG Act is that the administrative subpoena authority language of these laws is part of a narrow statutory scheme authorizing a specific agency to set particular policies or which otherwise amends a specific organic act to expand that agency's policymaking responsibilities. The administrative subpoena authority in the IG Act is agnostic of policymaking and, in fact, a single sentence, unspecific to any one agency, creates the subpoena power for all IGs. That is decidedly not the case with other administrative subpoena authorities delegated to the bureaucracy. In this sense, when administrative subpoena power is dependent upon a particularly policymaking scheme it functions as an administrative procedure limiting the scope of the agency's investigative jurisdiction. When subpoena power is independent from a particularly policymaking scheme, it functions as an administrative procedure delimiting constraints on policy jurisdiction and, in the process, controlling the acts of the policymaking officials.

Because the Inspector General Act sits within the same Title of the United States Code (Title 5) as other administrative procedure laws like the Administrative Procedure Act and the Freedom of Information Act, similar to inferences that can be made about the statutory placement of administrative subpoena powers, I can assess whether Congress more efficiently secures its oversight preferences by establishing permanent policy- and agency-agnostic administrative procedures governing congressional delegation of its regulatory powers to the bureaucracy rather than tailoring administrative procedures to particular policy prescriptions that are often subject to revision based on which party holds power.

I find strong causal evidence that in creating Inspectors General, Congress maximizes oversight efficiency by reducing its oversight workload and permitting members on committees with oversight jurisdiction to maximize their electoral interests through the publicity, position-taking, and credit-claiming that oversight hearings provide. This finding supports the explanatory significance of the investigative state by showing that Congress not only delegates the power to investigate, but it also delegates the fire-alarm monitoring itself by creating fire chiefs within the bureaucracy.

While administrative procedures governing official conduct enhances congressional oversight efficiency, administrative procedures constraining regulatory investigations to a policy domain do not affect oversight efficiency. A legal scholar might suggest these results show that when Congress empowers agencies to issue administrative subpoenas it simply abdicates legislative control because agencies use such subpoenas as part and parcel of law enforcement. Even if administrative subpoenas were relied upon by the bureaucracy for law enforcement purposes, evidence of an electoral connection between executive branch law enforcement and congressional oversight would not mean abdication. In my final empirical model, I assess the extent to which executive branch use of administrative subpoenas for law enforcement maximizes Congress's oversight efficiency. I develop a dataset coding all federal enforcement filings by the United States and model the effects of administrative subpoena authorizations, as instrumented through federal law enforcement, on Congress's preference to use congressional oversight to maximize its electoral incentives. While I find that the causal relationship between increases in federal law enforcement filings and increases in oversight efficiency is statistically significant, the substantive impact of the effect is negligible.[21] This should lead us to be skeptical that Congress maintains control over delegation to the bureaucracy of its compulsory investigative powers over the private sphere. Congress would appear to delegate its oversight over the executive branch while abdicating its powers to investigate the private sphere.

The finding that Congress prefers to statutorily delegate its political oversight powers to the bureaucracy, which enables members on committees with oversight authority to more efficiently advance their electoral interests, is a novel contribution to the political science literature. This conclusion follows from the evidence supporting four new principles informing the study of congressional oversight: first, while members may have competing preferences between *ex post* oversight via hearings versus *ex ante* oversight via statutory procedures, the legislative oversight power is itself the result of Congress's delegation of legislative authority; second, because oversight is a legislative power, that power can itself be delegated and Congress has, in fact, delegated that power; third, because of their electoral interests, committee members with oversight authority prefer to hold more oversight hearings with less time spent per hearing ("oversight efficiency"); and fourth, delegation of congressional oversight power to the bureaucracy increases oversight efficiency. In the chapters that follow, these findings become explicit through an examination of the relevant literature and the novel empirical strategy employed to investigate the relationship between delegation and oversight.

[21] As Model 4 in Table 7 in Appendix D (Chapter 4) shows, even when I weight the variables by standard deviation, we observe that to achieve just a single day increase in total annual oversight efficiency would require 17,000 law enforcement filings the previous year.

CHAPTER 2

The American Political History and Jurisprudence Behind Congressional Delegation of the Investigative Power

Political scientists[1] and administrative law scholars[2] recognize that Congress delegates its legislative authority to the bureaucracy and thus has a corresponding need to monitor how the bureaucracy implements policy through regulation.[3] Scholars describe oversight as this political monitoring of the bureaucracy. Yet Congress's investigative powers, described by scholars and policy actors as "oversight powers," have been used against non-bureaucrats: presidents, White House staff, cabinet secretaries, and corporate CEOs for reasons other than a need to monitor delegated authority in the form of regulation. Theories about oversight generally elude explaining congressional inquiries and hearings targeted at the private sector or toward the president and his appointees. The activities, particularly those of Congress, that are instead demarcated to involve oversight are investigations, hearings, administrative procedures, or special interest litigation focused on the regulatory activity of

[1] *See* Epstein & O'Halloran (1999a, b), *infra* at note 118, and note 8 in Chapter 3.

[2] Peter H. Aranson, Ernst Gelhorn, & Glen O. Robinson, *A Theory of Legislative Delegation*, 68 Cornell L. Rev. 1, 9 (1982).

[3] David Epstein & Sharyn O'Halloran, *Asymmetric Information, Delegation, and the Structure of Policy-Making*, 11 J. Theoretical Pol. 37 (1999) (Congress seeks to control delegated authority through administrative procedures, oversight, and administrative law) (hereinafter "Epstein & O'Halloran (1999c)).

D. Z. Epstein, *The Investigative State: Regulatory Oversight in the United States*, https://doi.org/10.1007/978-3-031-38461-5_2

the bureaucracy in the form of promulgated rules. Rules are of interest because they reflect the bureaucracy's power to act legislatively—rules, like statutes, have the force of law.

But just as Congress empowers agencies to "legislate" in the form of rules, Congress has also empowered the bureaucracy as it relates to other core legislative activities. These activities range from investigations of the private sector to impeachment inquiries directed at political appointees and the president. These activities raise the core research question of this book: whether Congress delegates these investigative powers in the same way that it delegates its rulemaking authority to the bureaucracy. Similar to Congress empowering the bureaucracy to legislate via rulemaking, I suspect that agency investigations of the private sphere and agency investigations of the political administration originate in the congressional choice to delegate authority to the bureaucracy. Oversight of the bureaucracy, as articulated above, involves congressional monitoring of the bureaucracy's exercise of its rulemaking power. But if Congress delegates investigative powers to the bureaucracy, an additional issue arises: We would expect Congress to monitor how the bureaucracy exercises Congress's own powers of inquiry. Does Congress do so?

These questions reveal the connection between delegation of legislative power to the bureaucracy and the corresponding interest by Congress in monitoring the exercise of that power through oversight. If Congress delegates more than just rules to the bureaucracy, then the scope of its oversight would similarly expand. And given this scope, I theorize that Congress would have incentives to rely on administrative procedures to monitor investigative inquiries carried out by the bureaucracy. As I show in this chapter, Title 5 of the United States Code provides stark evidence of how Congress establishes administrative procedures to monitor both bureaucratic rulemaking and bureaucratic investigations. Title 5 is more familiar to the general policy audience in the form of its many sections: the Freedom of Information Act, the Administrative Procedure Act, the Hatch Act, the Ethics in Government Act, the Federal Advisory Committee Act, and the Privacy Act. Title 5 also creates, beyond administrative procedures governing regulation, administrative officers ("fire chiefs" within the concept of "fire alarms") who help set the congressional oversight agenda. Of particular interest to this book are the Inspectors General, presidentially appointed bureaucrats statutorily empowered to investigate agency programs and operations but who, cautious to appease their congressional enablers, use their investigative authority to probe activities involving political appointees in an administration.

This chapter addresses the questions presented above by clarifying that legislative policymaking is more than legislative rulemaking and activities auxiliary to establishing rules, e.g., "bill sponsorship, committee markups, and recorded votes[.]"[4] For most of its history, Congress has also made policy through investigations and adjudications of citizen claims for payment by the government. And given this universe of legislative power, the delegation of policymaking to the bureaucracy would be expected to include more than the authority to write rules. Scholars tend to present the relationship between delegation of legislative power and oversight of that power in the context of legislative rulemaking, eschewing investigations, and adjudications by legislative agencies (e.g., the independent Federal Trade Commission) or officers (e.g., the Comptroller General) as complex and thorny powers secondary to, if not separate from, legislative power.

The legislative power to investigate is underdetermined by the contemporary image of oversight, for investigations are ancillary to the creation of legislation itself. As shown in this chapter, before Congress ever delegated to the bureaucracy its power to write laws, it delegated and oversaw the implementation of its investigative powers.[5] As Fig. 1 illustrates, when Congress investigated, adjudicated, and made rules without delegating those powers to the bureaucracy, its probes of presidential administrations were necessarily unattached to a legislative need to monitor implementation of legislative power ("Legislative investigations, 1789–1820"). Congress's investigations of the private sector at this point were informal information-gathering exercises used for the purposes of obtaining information in order to adjudicate a citizen's or contractor's claim to payment by the government and write a private bill directing the Treasury Department make the payment. During this time, the scope of congressional authority to regulate commerce was limited to establishing federal port districts to ensure states licensed and charged ships and their cargo fairly as they navigated colonial waters. As the country rapidly industrialized,

[4] *See e.g.*, James Valvo & Ryan P. Mulvey, *Government Transparency Is Fundamental*, Americans for Prosperity Foundation Blog (Mar. 15, 2021), *available at* https://americansforprosperity.org/government-transparency-is-fundamental/.

[5] *Wayman v. Southard*, 23 U.S. (10 Wheat.) 1, 43 (1825) ("Congress may certainly delegate to others, powers which the legislature may rightfully exercise itself").

the invention of the railroad and the conversion of an agrarian labor economy to formation of the urban, industrialized labor class forced the provincial notion of commerce among the several states to yield to an expanded power over "interstate commerce."[6] To address these national pressures, Congress aggressively investigated the private sector and subsequently passed laws establishing the federal bureaucracy empowered with Congress's adjudicative and investigative powers, but where Congress retained its rulemaking powers[7] ("Legislative investigations, 1820–1946").

Only when Congress authorized rulemaking by the bureaucracy, while simultaneously empowering the executive departments to make policy rather than simply enforce the law under the president's supervision, does the contemporary concept of oversight arise ("Legislative investigations, 1946-present"). At this point of history, virtually every aspect of legislative power was exercised by the executive branch in some form. The delegation of legislative powers to investigate, and, finally, the power to write laws, simultaneously created the administrative state and necessitated the modern concept of oversight.

This chapter shows that in addition to administrative rulemaking, administrative investigations are part of bureaucratic policymaking. Both political scientists and administrative law scholars err in limiting congressional delegation to the bureaucracy to administrative rulemaking.[8] The legislative power, its delegation, and its subsequent oversight are all broader than mere rulemaking.

[6] *See* E.E. Schattschneider, *The Semisovereign People: A Realist's View of Democracy in America* (1960) at 119.

[7] Abraham Ribicoff, *Congressional Oversight and Regulatory Reform*, 28 Administrative L. Rev. (1976) at 416.

[8] Yackee & Yackee, *supra* note 1 in Chapter 3 at 400 ("The recognition that agencies can write rules reflects Congress's ability to delegate to agencies the power to regulate, while the requirement to reference the legal authority to do so reflects the fact that agencies may not regulate absent such delegation."); *accord*. Cary Coglianese & Daniel E. Walters, *Agenda-Setting in the Regulatory State: Theory and Evidence*, 68 Administrative L. Rev. 865, 868 (2016).

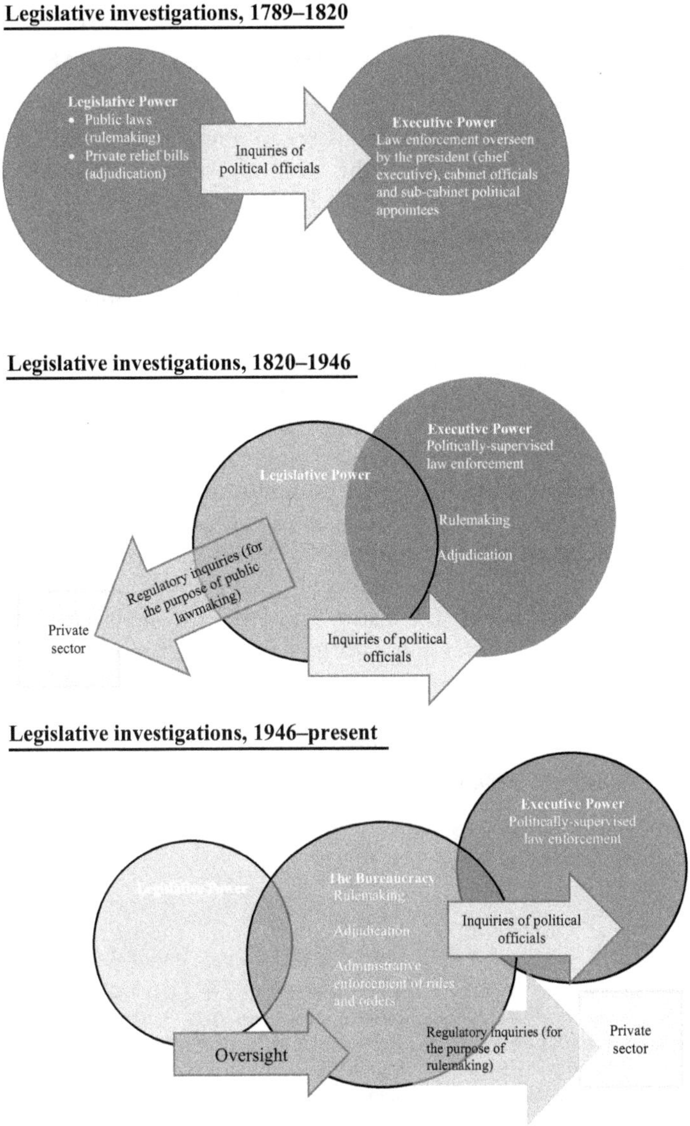

Fig. 1 Models of legislative and executive power over time

1 The Legislative Power to Investigate and Its Delegation to the Executive Branch

McNollGast have argued that administrative law is "written for the purpose of helping elected politicians retain control of policymaking."[9] In particular, they argue that "the legal constraints imposed in the Administrative Procedure[] Act (APA) and elsewhere enable political officials to overcome certain informational inequalities between themselves and administrative officers."[10] For administrative law scholars, agencies make policies ("agency action") either through rules applied to a class of persons ("rulemaking") or specific orders binding individual parties ("adjudication").[11] These scholars and the Supreme Court have described rulemaking as a "legislative" power and adjudication as a "judicial" power. When political scientists discuss "administrative procedures" they mean the legislative requirements governing rulemaking or adjudication. Indeed, in their discussion of the Administrative Procedure Act and other administrative procedures, McNollGast reduce agency policymaking choices to "rulemaking and adjudication."[12] Further McNollGast argue that administrative procedures reduce "informational costs" associated with oversight and enable "fire-alarm" monitoring, where constituencies affected by agency policies can inform Congress of agency drift from legislative intent.[13]

Noticeably absent from this literature is the identification of congressional investigations as part of Congress's legislative power and therefore the bureaucracy's investigations of both the private sphere and political

[9] McNollGast 1987, *supra* note 5 in Chapter 3 at *id.*

[10] *Id.*

[11] Further the choice of policy procedure is considered to be in the discretion of the agency. *See* Aaron Nielson, *Beyond Seminole Rock*, 105 Geo. L. J. 943, 948 (2017). Administrative law scholars rely on the Supreme Court's statement that "an administrative agency must be equipped to act either by general rule or by individual order. To insist upon one form of action to the exclusion of the other is to exalt form over necessity." *SEC v. Chenery Corp.*, 332 U.S. 194, 202 (1947) (known as "Chenery II").

[12] McNollGast 1987, *supra* note 5 in Chapter 3 at 262.

[13] *Id.* at 273 (referencing Mathew McCubbins & Thomas Schwartz, *Congressional Oversight Overlooked: Police Patrols vs. Fire Alarms*, 28 Am. J. of Pol. Sci. (1984) at 165–179).

officials are either unexamined or dismissed from the scope of congressional oversight, as activities outside of rulemaking or adjudication.[14] Executive branch scholars' omission of investigations from the scope of legislative policymaking is followed by Congress scholars. For instance, Kriner and Schwartz describe "congressional investigations" as policing the executive branch through "nonlegislative means".[15] As I show in this chapter, Congress's history as an institution reflects congressional investigations of political officials (the "administration"), executive agencies (the "bureaucracy"), and the private sector, as well as its adjudicatory functions, to be as essential to the legislative power, if not more so, than is Congress's power to write laws.[16]

The first research question I seek to address is whether Congress delegates its investigative powers to the bureaucracy or is simply authorizing the bureaucracy to conduct investigations as law enforcement activities. The distinction between delegation versus authorization matters to constitutional debates about the separation of powers, for if Congress is simply authorizing a department or agency to subpoena for information, there is no reason to suspect that the agency is exercising a "legislative" power versus one consistent with executive branch authority. Delegated legislative powers, however, do not suddenly become "executive" when exercised by agency heads. This constitutional gloss matters for political scientists because the distinction between authorization and delegation has implications for explaining whether *ex post* monitoring of agency infractions is causally related to the exercise of legislative power by the agency or wholly unrelated. When Congress delegates, rather than merely authorizes, agency authority will be subject to administrative procedures "which may dictate the policy-making process that agencies must follow,

[14] McNollGast 1987, *supra* note 5 in Chapter 3 at 245 (identifying the source of policymaking as "legislation or executive order").

[15] Kriner & Schwartz, *supra* note 19 in Chapter 3 at 297.

[16] J. William Fulbright, *Congressional Investigations: Significance for the Legislative Process*, 18 U. Chi. L. Rev. 440, 441 (1951) (describing the congressional power of inquiry as "perhaps the most necessary of all the powers underlying the legislative function").

empower certain constituents to influence agency decisions, or circumscribe permissible agency actions" or reporting requirements (to, e.g., congressional committees, GAO), or both.[17]

Historical evidence shows Congress's policymaking power includes investigations of the private sphere and investigations of presidential administration. The relevant historical and legislative materials support a broad understanding of legislative power, inclusive of a number of the sorts of powers legal scholars tend to conceive of as committed to the executive or judicial departments. Judicial doctrine has recognized these broad legislative powers and their delegation in the creation of the administrative state. Epstein and O'Halloran model the congressional decision to delegate as a discrete choice from the alternative decision to do more work in-house.[18] This model assumes, however, that observable congressional policy work is not somehow causally determined by agenda-setting that occurs when delegees of legislative power pull fire alarms or otherwise send information back to their congressional principals. In using historical evidence to inform my empirical models, I show that Congress, in creating the administrative state, delegated its investigative powers together with its power to write rules as a conscious strategy to enhance political capacity: maximize the ideological value of its policy work while minimizing any policy work that is resource-intensive yet of minimal electoral value.

Political scientists understand delegation on a statute-by-statute basis versus through Congress using broad enactments that authorize a range of agency action over time. For instance, Epstein and O'Halloran show that Congress writes more detailed tax rules but defers to the executive branch on environmental rules. This understanding of delegation,

[17] Epstein & O'Halloran (1999c), *supra* note 3 at 41. While beyond the scope of this book, many legal scholars suggest that all agencies within the executive branch are "executive agencies" and thus whether they engage in adjudication or rulemaking, agency action is always executive versus legislative or judicial in nature. For these scholars, Congress can bind executive law enforcement through administrative procedures. A normative implication of this book is that Congress cannot conduct oversight (whether through administrative procedures or hearings) of purely executive decisions. In the case of agency action subject to administrative procedure, those functions are not law enforcement and therefore well within Congress' oversight authority. Indeed if rulemaking was truly part of an inherent executive power it would mean Congress had the authority to cabin the president's law enforcement discretion.

[18] *Id.*

however, is only partially explained by electoral incentives but more fully understandable in terms of legislative capacity enhanced when delegation ensures Congress has a stream of policy information over time. Surely it is possible that Congress at one point treated tax policy like environmental policy, relying on the executive branch to fill in the policy details until, at some point of time, Congress developed the capacity to write tax rules more efficiently. This notion of congressional learning presents a model of delegation and oversight as causally linked by a bureaucracy that sets the policy agenda of Congress.[19]

1.1 The Legislative Power to Investigate

Executive branch scholarship overlooks the fact that before Congress ever delegated its power to make rules, it delegated its investigative powers.[20] This fact is crucial to understanding both the political development of congressional delegation and its relationship to political oversight over that delegation. Models that interpret delegation as evidence of the congressional lack of expertise to regulate modern economies overlook historical reality. That reality reflects Congress's initial decision to delegate legislative power due to the expansion of Congress's policy mandate and the need for permanent entities insulated from politics to police theretofore unregulated private sector conduct. In fact, the evidence reflects a deliberate decision by Congress to delegate adjudicative and investigative powers while retaining its rule-writing authority, insisting that agencies

[19] The administrative state, by design, has the bureaucracy assist Congress in forming legislative policy. *See* Nicholas R. Parrillo, *Leviathan and Interpretive Revolution: The Administrative State, the Judiciary, and the Rise of Legislative History, 1890–1950*, 123 Yale L.J. 266, 333 ("the agencies and DOJ divisions constantly communicated and negotiated with Congress on how to administer (and whether to amend) the statutes in their charge, and legislative history was essential to that work—something that drove the agencies and DOJ not merely to collect legislative history, but to collect it in 'real time,' which was the most efficient way"). This historical evidence provides additional reasons to dismiss Epstein and O'Halloran's discrete choice model—in any model of congressional committees deciding to delegate less by writing detailed rules, the committees are able to direct the assistant of the bureaucracy in the rule-writing process. In fact, the practice of the bureaucracy writing legislation is called "technical assistance." *See* Admin. Conf. of the U.S., Recommendation 2015-2, Technical Assistance by Federal Agencies in the Legislative Process, 80 Fed. Reg. 78161 (Dec. 16, 2015).

[20] *Humphrey's Executor*, note 37, *infra*.

report their investigative findings back to Congress in order to enable more intelligible regulations of business by the legislature.

For those scholars who frame the study of oversight of the bureaucracy within the context of delegation, it is necessary to recognize that the administrative state began with Congress's limited delegation of its adjudicative and investigative powers[21] and only after decades of constitutional litigation paralleling economic panics and post-industrial revolution conflict, did Congress empower agencies to make rules and regulations.[22] This historical perspective coheres with Epstein and O'Halloran's finding that a lack of congressional capacity to write technically demanding policy cannot explain the congressional choice to delegate. Relying upon that history, this section illustrates that the administrative subpoena power of the bureaucracy originated with Congress's own power to investigate and thus should be understood as a delegation of policymaking, not inherent law enforcement power.

Agency investigations, like their congressional forbears, should be understood as intrinsic to the bureaucracy's ability to effectively write rules with the force of law. Because administrative law scholars and scholars of Congress and the executive branch overlook the narrow original context in which Congress delegated its power, contemporary regulatory authority is classified as either rulemaking—where the activity must relate to the rule development process—or everything else, with investigations, permit applications, and discretionary grant evaluations all being classified as "adjudication." The attempt to gloss a muddled historical understanding with legal clarity has led to mistaking agency investigations as the sorts of constitutional law enforcement subject to presidential supervision while at the same time motivating the impulse, seen in modern presidential administrations, to treat the bureaucracy as inherently executive in its functions. Without understanding the historical

[21] *Ex parte Bakelite Corp.*, 279 U.S. 438, 452 (1929) (the power "to examine and determine claims for money against the United States ... is a function which belongs primarily to Congress as an incident of its power to pay the debts of the United States. But the function is one which Congress has a discretion either to exercise directly or to delegate to other agencies").

[22] *See* Interstate Commerce Act, note 42, *infra*. Note also that the 1914 Federal Trade Commission Act, 63 P.L. 203, §(g) established the FTC's rulemaking powers, which were limited in application to activities leading up to a complaint as, § 5 makes clear that once the commission issues an order, it can only be enforced by a federal circuit court.

and political dependency of legislative rule-writing on regulatory investigations, the scope of regulatory power and its oversight are unnecessarily limited.

The Congressional Power to Investigate Political Officials
The first several congressional inquiries by select committees directed toward the George Washington administration were not aimed at contemporary legal justifications like legislation or impeachment but toward what then-Representative James Madison in 1790 described as a need to "possess itself of the fullest information in order to do[] justice to the country and to public officers."[23] And certainly the first century-and-a-half of Congresses did not issue subpoenas to executive branch officials or succeed in holding such officials in contempt[24] although compulsory process and contempt was in fact successfully directed toward individuals and corporations.[25]

Two inherent contempt proceedings against executive branch officials occurred in the first century-and-a-half since the Founding. In 1879, State Department official George Seward was arrested by the Sergeant-at-Arms of the U.S. House of Representatives, yet was eventually released on grounds that the legislative purpose—impeachment—was sufficiently quasi-criminal to prevent Seward's being forced to self-incriminate. In 1916, the House Sergeant-at-Arms arrested U.S. Attorney for the Southern District of New York H. Snowden Marshall under the presumption that Marshall had engaged in "high crimes and misdemeanors." However, the Supreme Court invalidated the use of contempt, drawing a distinction between the right use of the power for "self-preservation" and the wrong use as the equivalent of a "law for punishment for wrongful acts."[26]

[23] 2 Annals of Cong. 1514 (Mar. 19, 1790) at 1515.

[24] *See generally* Louis Fisher, *Congressional Access to Executive Branch Information: Legislative Tools*, Congressional Research Service Report, *available at* https://fas.org/sgp/crs/secrecy/RL30966.pdf#page=26. Note that only two contempts of executive officials occurred from 1789 to 1916 and both failed to be fully enforced.

[25] *Anderson v. Dunn*, 6 Wheat. (19 U.S.) 204, 228 (1821).

[26] *Marshall v. Gordon*, 243 U.S. 521, 546 (1917).

The lesson from these episodes is two-fold: first, Congress has the authority to investigate the president and his political appointees (copartisans) under its impeachment power but second, these political investigations are not enforceable by the courts. Rather than Congress using the courts to redress resistance or noncompliance by the president and his copartisans with congressional inquiries, Congress can secure a political remedy through its own procedures or rely on the party or the media to attack the administration for noncompliance with an inquiry. Such political pressure has consequences: the president is removable through the electoral process, the president can be pressured to fire his appointees, or the president and any official, including judges, can be removed through impeachment. To illustrate this principle, on November 24, 1800, the president accepted the resignation of Secretary of the Treasury Wolcott due to congressional criticisms of his administration, leading one congressman to state that "an inquiry [] made into [] official conduct … will operate as a general stimulus to the faithful discharge of duty."[27] Judicial review would be thought to deprive the political branches of these electoral tools.[28]

That political inquiries by Congress were authorized but not judicially enforceable was the longstanding position of the executive branch from the Founding until the Nixon presidency. In a 1941 letter by then-Attorney General (and future Supreme Court Justice) Robert Jackson to Representative Carl Vinson, the Chairman of the House Committee on Naval Affairs, Jackson denied the Committee access to reports of the Federal Bureau of Investigation. Attorney General Jackson's denial of congressional access to information assessed the information's legislative value, concluding, "[t]he information here involved was collected, and is chiefly valuable, for use by the executive branch of the Government in the execution of the laws. It can be of little, if any, value in connection with the framing of legislation or the performance of any other constitutional

[27] 10 Ann. Cong. 786, 788 (1800).

[28] *Baker v. Carr*, 369 U.S. 186, 217 (1962). *See e.g., Cummings v. Murphy*, 321 F. Supp. 3d 92, 101–102 (D.D.C. 2018) (concerns about the "'properly limited role of the courts in a democratic society … are particularly acute' where, as here, 'a legislator attempts to bring an essentially political dispute into a judicial forum'") (citing *Chenoweth v. Clinton*, 181 F.3d 112, 114 (D.C. Cir. 1999) (internal citations omitted)).

duty of the Congress."[29] Further, Jackson rehearsed the constitutional zeitgeist of the time that "[t]he courts have repeatedly held that they will not and cannot require the executive to produce such papers when in the opinion of the executive their production is contrary to the public interests. The courts have also held that the question whether the production of the papers would be against the public interest is one for the executive and not for the courts to determine."[30] Jackson's position in 1941 mirrored President Washington's determination in 1792 concerning the House inquiry into General St. Clair's military defeat: provide the House with those papers as the "public good would permit and [] refuse those the disclosure of which would harm the public."[31]

After President Nixon's impeachment, the federal courts determined that disputes between Congress and executive branch officials are not merely political when Congress is able to show institutional harm resulting from the executive branch's noncompliance with a duly issued congressional subpoena.[32] In the context of the American politics literature, the courts have overlooked the political nature of oversight in order to artificially create legislative legal capacity over the administration.[33] While congressional policymaking in the form of legislation requires the affirmative consent of the president, "congressional oversight, at least initially, requires that only the legislative branch act."[34]

29 *Position of the Executive Department Regarding Investigative Reports*, 40 Op. Att'y Gen. 45, 60 (1941) (hereinafter "Jackson Opinion").

30 *See* Jackson Opinion, *supra* note 29 at 49.

31 George C. Chalou, *St. Clair's Defeat, 1792*, in Arthur M. Schlesinger, Jr., ed., Congress Investigates: A Documented History, 1792–1974 (1983) at 4.

32 *Committee on the Judiciary v. Miers*, 558 F. Supp. 2d 55, 68 (D.D.C. 2008); *United States v. AT&T*, 551 F.2d 384, 391 (D.C. Cir. 1976) ("It is clear that the House as a whole has standing to assert its investigatory power, and can designate a member to act on its behalf.").

33 "[I]ndividual members of the Congress lack standing to assert the institutional interests of a legislature in the same way a single House of a bicameral legislature lacks capacity to assert interests belonging to the legislature as a whole." *Blumenthal et al. v. Trump*, No. 17-cv-01154 at *9 (D.C. Cir. 2020) (citing *Va. House of Delegates v. Bethune-Hill*, 139 S. Ct. 1945, 1953–54 (2019)) (internal citations omitted).

34 CRS Report to Congress, *The Debate over Selected Presidential Assistants and Advisors: Appointment, Accountability, and Congressional Oversight*, Report No. R40856 (2014) at 44.

The Congressional Power to Investigate the Private Sphere

In its first half-century, Congress passed both public and private acts[35] and the earliest congressional standing committees, like the House Committee on Commerce and Manufactures and the Committee on Claims, engaged in investigative powers in reviewing private petitions for the purpose of enacting resolutions and private laws.[36] The first time Congress subjected its compulsory process power to bicameralism and presentment was not as part of any investigation of the government but for empowering its committees to adjudicate petitions by private parties.[37] The first century-and-a-half of standing committee investigations involved inquiries to corporations for purposes of informing both private bills and regulations of interstate commerce, where requests for testimony and documents could be compelled and enforced.[38] Contrary to popular views that the administrative state is the result of Woodrow Wilson's progressivism[39] or Franklin D. Roosevelt's "New Deal,"[40] the administrative state began as the legislative result of committee investigations of railroads, depots, ports, and the businesses that profited from them.[41]

[35] *See e.g.*, President George Washington's bound copy of the Acts passed by the First Congress, *available at* http://catalog.mountvernon.org/digital/collection/p16829coll5/id/841.

[36] National Archives and Records Administration, Records of the Committee on Commerce and Manufactures (1795–1819), *available at* https://www.archives.gov/legislative/guide/house/chapter-07.html#CmtCommerceManu1795.

[37] Testimony in Private Claims, 20 Stat. 278, 45 Cong. Ch. 40 (Feb. 3, 1879). *See* Farah Peterson, *Expounding the Constitution*, 130 Yale L.J. 2, 16 (2020) (discussing that the number of private bills dwarfed the number of public laws in the Founding era).

[38] *See* "Subpoena Power and Contempt" in History, Art and Archives of the U.S. House of Representatives, "Investigations & Oversight", *available at* https://history.house.gov/Institution/Origins-Development/Investigations-Oversight/ (note that even this publication by the U.S. House of Representatives makes a distinction between "investigat[ing] issues that may require legislation in the future" and "investigat[ing] and oversee[ing] federal programs").

[39] Christopher DeMuth, *Can the Administrative State Be Tamed?* 8 J. of Legal Analysis (2016) at 157 (tracing the administrative state's "origins in the Progressive Era").

[40] Gary Lawson, *The Rise and Rise of the Administrative State*, 107 Harv. L. Rev. (1994) at 1231.

[41] "1885–1886 Select Committee to Investigate Interstate Commerce," U.S. Senate, *A History of Notable Senate Investigations*, *available at* https://www.senate.gov/artandhistory/history/common/briefing/Investigations.htm.

1.2 Delegation Beyond Rules

Congress Has Delegated to the Bureaucracy the Legislative Power to Investigate the Private Sector

The historical distinction between the role of Congress and its committees as both publicly regulating and privately adjudicating is a necessary background to the congressional practice that followed. The Interstate Commerce Act of 1887, in creating the Interstate Commerce Commission (ICC), represented the first time Congress granted "law enforcement" powers directly to an agency head (or board) rather than a single constitutionally appointed officer who could be removed by the president at will. Over time, the Supreme Court concluded that "enforcement" agencies like the ICC (and its descendants like the FTC or SEC) lacked law enforcement power and were simply exercising delegated legislative power. Foreshadowing this distinction between law enforcement and policy enforcement, the first national law enforcement statute, the Judiciary Act of 1789, was authorized under Congress's ability to empower the executive to enforce the law via the Necessary & Proper Clause ("Congress shall have Power ... To make all Laws which shall be necessary and proper for carrying into Execution the foregoing Powers[ ]"). The ICC's investigative powers, however, were justified under the Commerce Clause ("Congress shall have Power ... To regulate Commerce ... among the several states[ ]").

Like the nineteenth-century Congress itself, the ICC had to rely on the Attorney General to enforce its subpoenas by seeking relief from a court; self-enforcing legislative power, as observed in the cases of Seward and Marshall, was thought to violate the Constitution. At this point of time, Congress, most visibly through the Committees on Commerce and Manufactures in both houses, continued to directly engage in the use of investigative powers for purposes of determining the nation's legislative needs, which was separate from the enforcement powers it granted to executive officers. The distinction is governed by the understanding that Congress had no constitutional power to self-enforce its requests for information in court—it had only the self-enforcing contempt power or the ability to recommend the seeking of judicial relief from, and rely on the discretion of, the U.S. Attorneys and the Attorney General.

The blurring of the line between legislative inquiries and enforcement inquiries begins with the history of legislative changes and Supreme Court decisions concerning the ICC. The 1887 Interstate Commerce

Act provided no legislative rulemaking authority to the ICC but simply declared discrimination in rail rates to be unlawful.[42] The only rules the Commission could promulgate were rules applying to adjudications.[43] The Commission was empowered to act in a similar manner to the Select Committee to Investigate Interstate Commerce, which could subpoena corporations and obtain judicial compliance with those subpoenas. Congress, in creating the first administrative agency, delegated its investigative and adjudicatory authority but not its rulemaking authority, instead establishing the requirement that the Commission furnish Congress with a report which "shall contain such information and data collected by the Commission as may be considered of value in the determination of questions connected with the regulation of commerce, together with such recommendations as to additional legislation relating thereto as the Commission may deem necessary."[44]

The mistake made by contemporary scholars is to assume that legislation which empowers investigative authority without rulemaking authority is not delegation at all but simply a grant of law enforcement power to the executive. The Select Committee to Investigate Interstate Commerce could only obtain judicial relief for its investigations of the private sector (versus nonjusticiable investigations for impeachment purposes). Congress, in creating the Interstate Commerce Commission, effectively cloned the Select Committee with the only palpable difference being the ICC having statutory permanence whereas the Select Committee's existence depended upon reestablishment during each session of Congress. Reporting requirements to Congress including "recommendations as to additional legislation" first arose in the context of congressional delegation, to an executive agency, of its investigatory power over individuals and commerce. It is arguable that the early Supreme Court's recognition of "ministerial duties" with which Congress could obligate executive branch officials to carry out various responsibilities, is what made possible the assignment of such duties to an entire agency.

For the next several decades, Congress would still directly investigate political officials and programs. But the idea of congressional delegation to an agency vested with expertise so as to reduce the resource burden of

[42] 24 Stat. 379 §§ 2–5 (1887).

[43] *Id.* at § 17.

[44] *Id.* at § 21.

Congress was well-established half-a-century before the New Deal. What is contemporarily described as the congressional oversight power—where Congress monitors how agencies exercise delegated authority—first arises in the context of Congress looking to the bureaucracy to conduct the fact-gathering necessary for legislation. This early idea of fact-gathering (investigations) to inform regulation is precisely what undergirds the notion of a "legislative purpose" in contemporary congressional oversight jurisprudence.

In 1903, Congress and the president enacted the Hepburn Act, which amended the Interstate Commerce Act of 1887 to clarify that the ICC was an "independent agency" and thus not subject to presidential supervision.[45] The Hepburn Act's 1903 amendments to the Interstate Commerce Act formed the textual Adam's rib for the creation of all subsequent "independent enforcement" agencies that make up the modern American federal bureaucracy: initially the Federal Trade Commission and the U.S. Department of Labor, and over the decades, every subsequent policy enforcement commission, i.e., the Securities and Exchange Commission and the Commodities Futures Trading Commission.

In *Oklahoma Press Publishing v. Walling* the Supreme Court summed up these historical developments in describing the administrative subpoenas used by bureaucracies to investigate the private sector as "delegated power"[46] by Congress "incidental to both [Congress's] general legislative and its investigative powers."[47] *Oklahoma Press Publishing* was decided in the same year President Truman signed the Administrative Procedure Act. In the *Oklahoma Press* case, the Supreme Court was confronted with a challenge to the enforcement of a subpoena issued by the U.S. Department of Labor's Wage and Hour Division pursuant to Section 11(a) of the Fair Labor Standards Act (FLSA) on grounds that paralleled challenges to congressional inquiries: the FLSA does not cover or apply to the conduct alleged to be in violation. The *Oklahoma Press* Court could have easily resolved the circuit split (between the Tenth and Third Circuits) with a simple *per curiam* opinion applying its prior holding in *Endicott Johnson*. This fact, in addition to the timing of the Court's decision-making, notes from Justice Stone to Justice Rutledge

[45] 32 Stat. 847 (1903).

[46] *Oklahoma Press Publishing v. Walling*, 327 U.S. 186, 194–195.

[47] *Oklahoma Press*, *id.* at 214.

indicating the opinion was written in 1945 but held until after the Senate passed the final version of the Administrative Procedure Act,[48] and the fact that Justice Jackson, who helped write the Administrative Procedure Act, was recused, reflects the strategic considerations behind the Stone Court's insulating regulatory inquiries from APA review.

It is reasonable to speculate that Justice Jackson may have recused himself from *Oklahoma Press* because he, as former Attorney General, was the lead author of the 1941 report to the president on Administrative Procedure (which summarized the Republicans' various legislative attempts, most prominently the Walter-Logan bill, at constraining the New Deal regulatory state). In the 1941 report, then-Attorney General Jackson states a clear view as to how he would have decided *Oklahoma Press*, for when discussing the U.S. Department of Labor (DOL) (defendant in *Oklahoma Press Publishing*) and the Fair Labor Standards Act (FLSA) of 1938 (the statute at issue in *Oklahoma Press*) specifically, he wrote that administrative subpoenas should be issued as part of formal adjudications, not from law enforcement officers.[49] The Justice Murphy dissent in *Oklahoma Press* is of significance not only because of its content but because the 1941 Attorney General report on the Administrative Procedure Act to the president was requested by FDR in 1939—when Frank Murphy was Attorney General. After the final version of the APA passed the Senate, the Court then released the opinion in *Oklahoma Press* before Truman signed the statute, thus creating a presumption, still held today, that pre-complaint bureaucratic investigations are law enforcement activities committed to agency discretion and therefore not subject to the APA's rulemaking requirements. The idea that the APA ought to have overturned *Oklahoma Press* on this point has never been considered by the Court nor any of the advocates who set its agenda.

Congressional Delegation of the Legislative Power to Make Rules over the Private Sector Presumes a Prior Delegation of the Legislative Power to Investigate

In response to continuing public pressure concerning the increasing power of railroads, their holding companies, and the impact on industrial

[48] *See e.g.*, http://3197d6d14b5f19f2f440-5e13d29c4c016cf96cbbfd197c579b45.r81.cf1.rackcdn.com/collection/papers/1940/1945_1218_StoneRutledgeT.pdf.

[49] 1941 Attorney General's Report on Administrative Procedure at 150–151, *available at* http://archive.law.fsu.edu/library/admin/pdfdownload/apa1941.pdf#page=150.

workers, Congress, most prominently from 1903 to 1910, delegated its rulemaking powers over the private sphere to agencies. Up until this time, the regulation of industry was carried out by congressional investigations from 1789 to 1887 and executive branch investigations from 1887 to 1902. The federal administrative state which formed in the early twentieth century was preceded by a federal investigative state. It took nearly two decades after the creation of the ICC before Congress empowered it to "prescribe the forms of any and all accounts, records, and memoranda to be kept by carriers subject to the provisions of this Act."[50] This represented the first time in American history that Congress delegated the power to make rules with the force of law to an agency formally located within the executive branch.

The "administrative" state as conceived by scholars today was largely born from 1903 to 1914, primarily in the authority granted to the ICC, by empowering the investigative state with implementation (rulemaking) powers in order to interpret and enforce statutes. Before that time, Congress had withheld delegation of its rulemaking power in recognizing, as the *Humphrey's Executor* Court did, that agency investigations (just like congressional investigations of the private sector) were ancillary to the rulemaking activity of Congress. For instance, before the Federal Trade Commission (FTC) was delegated rulemaking power, the Supreme Court recognized that the FTC's investigative powers were limited in being subject to the "pursuance of a resolution of the Senate passed on August 9, 1921."[51] At the time, the FTC, like the ICC before it,[52] was dependent upon Congress for its policy agenda while subject to robust reporting requirements so that agency investigations of the private sector could inform congressional rule-writing.[53] Delegation of regulatory power to the executive became necessary and proper only in the context of an executive already vested with investigative and adjudicative powers.

[50] 34 Stat. 584 at § 20.

[51] *FTC v. American Tobacco Co.*, 264 U.S. 268 (1924).

[52] FTC investigations against corporations were dependent upon authorization pursuant to Senate resolutions. *See United States v. Louisville & N. R. Co.*, 236 U.S. 318, 324 (1915) (regarding the Interstate Commerce Commission).

[53] *Id.* at 303.

While Congress first delegated its investigative powers to the executive branch in 1887,[54] it was not until 1946 that Congress established a permanent committee system to oversee those delegated powers and establish procedures governing how the administrators of those powers regulated the public. The "oversight" most commonly studied by political scientists arises in 1946 as a distinct institution from prior committee investigations of the private sphere tied to rulemaking or adjudication or inquiries directed toward political officials overseeing executive departments.[55] *See* Fig. 1.

Unlike congressional investigations of political officials or the private sphere, "oversight" arises in response to the Congress ceding its legislative authority to administrative agencies.[56] Three decades after the Legislative Reorganization Act of 1946, Congress acknowledged that "[g]iven the broad delegations to the agencies…. The American system of representation imposes a responsibility on the Congress and the president to maintain popular control over the regulatory agencies. The regulatory process should be one in which regulators who exercise delegated authority are ultimately answerable to the people. Our study accepts as a premise that regulatory 'failure' is less likely to occur when Congress exercises effective oversight."[57] This observation is echoed by scholars who suggest that "[b]ecause public-policy issues are so complex, Congress has had to delegate authority over them to a large, complex, technically expert bureaucracy, whose actions it is unable effectively to oversee."[58]

54 *See e.g.*, Senate Resolution 71, "To Authorize a Study of the Purpose and Current Effectiveness of Federal Agencies", the Senate Committee on Government Operations issued Volume II of its "Study on Federal Regulation" titled "Congressional Oversight of Regulatory Agencies", 95th Cong. Sess. 2 at 15 (February 1977) (hereinafter "Senate Government Operations report").

55 Organization of the Congress, Reports of the Joint Committee on the Organization of Congress. 79th Cong., 2d sess., Rept. No. 1011, at 6 (Mar. 4, 1946).

56 *Id.*

57 Senate Government Operations report (1977), *supra* note 54 at 5.

58 McCubbins & Schwartz, *supra* note 5 in Chapter 3 at 169 (citing Lowi, 1969; Ogul, 1977; Ripley, 1969; Seidman, 1975; Woll, 1977).

Congress Delegates' Political Monitoring of Administration Appointees by Creating Bureaucratic Oversight Officials

While Supreme Court jurisprudence provides strong indicia that bureaucratic investigations of the private sector enforced via administrative subpoenas are delegations of Congress's same investigative authority, the political nature of impeachment investigations has meant a lack of judicial consideration of whether the congressional power to probe political officials has similarly been delegated to the bureaucracy.[59] I expect that the same motivations that cause Congress to delegate policymaking authority to the bureaucracy *writ large* would also apply to its power to probe impeachable administration officials. In other words, I expect there to be evidence that just as the bureaucracy writes rules and investigates the private sector, so too will the bureaucracy investigate political officials and these delegations create the need for congressional oversight. My particular interest is the creation of Inspectors General at each presidentially supervised department.

Through its impeachment power, Congress has the power to investigate political officials in the public interest. The legislative power to investigate executive branch political officials was not historically enforceable through subpoenas or contempt. It was within the president's discretion whether compliance was in the public interest.[60] Congress is always possessed of the remedy of impeachment and the public, with the electoral process. The Office of Legal Counsel takes the position, alluded to earlier, that in *United States v. Nixon*, the Supreme Court invalidated 185 years of precedent by holding that "the president's general privilege of confidentiality did not extend to an absolute privilege of immunity

[59] *See House Committees' Authority to Investigate for Impeachment*, 44 O.L.C., slip. op. 1, 10 (Jan. 19, 2020) ("The Constitution vests in the House of Representatives a share of Congress's legislative power and, separately, 'the sole Power of Impeachment.' U.S. Const. art. I, § 1; id. art. I, § 2, cl. 5. Both the legislative power and the impeachment power include an implied authority to investigate, including by means of compulsory process. But those investigative powers are not interchangeable. The House has broadly delegated to committees its power to investigate for legislative purposes, but it has held impeachment authority more closely, granting authority to conduct particular impeachment investigations only as the need has arisen.").

[60] *See* Jackson Opinion, *supra* note 29 (citing the history of executive branch refusals to comply with an inquiry as not in the "public interest" and clarifying that such denials were not justiciable).

from all judicial process."[61] *Nixon* is distinguishable from contemporary cases of interbranch disputes in that the dispute was narrowly limited to "the enforcement of a subpoena for confidential Presidential communications for use in a criminal prosecution[.]"[62] The holding in *Nixon* thus has nothing to do with congressional oversight or a dispute between the executive branch and Congress. Further *Nixon's* reasoning is seriously flawed, for in determining that the nation's chief law enforcement officer could be investigated by an inferior law enforcement official, it held "[s]ince this Court has consistently exercised the power to construe and delineate claims arising under express powers, it must follow that the Court has authority to interpret claims with respect to powers alleged to derive from enumerated powers."[63]

Because there is widespread scholarly agreement that Congress can delegate its legislative powers, the legal limitations applied to legislative powers as delegated should guide academic arguments about the appropriate limits on the use of such legislative powers directly by Congress. As Fig. 1 illustrates, congressional investigations of individuals and corporations from the early nineteenth century until the twentieth century were justified as necessary to establish regulatory agencies under the Commerce Clause. It is from this practice that the Supreme Court justified congressional investigations of individuals when made for a legitimate lawmaking purpose. But if this sense of regulatory purpose binds investigations of the executive branch as well, one would expect that chief executives would force Congress to clarify, consistent with the historical practice, what regulatory agency or regulatory scheme it sought to establish or reform on the basis of a given request for information or testimony.

Yet Congress has never—and does not—establish procedures to obtain information from the executive branch for the purposes of legislating *against* the executive branch. Instead, the procedure requiring the articulation by Congress of a "legitimate legislative purpose" for an investigation has been limited to Congress's legislative interest in regulating the private sector.[64] And Congress can enforce its private sector investigations through subpoenas and seek further compliance in the courts. On paper,

[61] 418 U.S. 683 (1974).

[62] *Nixon*, 418 U.S. at 703.

[63] *Id.* at 704.

[64] *Trump v. Mazars USA, LLP*, 140 S. Ct. 2019, 2048 (2020).

this is not the case with congressional investigations of political officials.[65] While Congress cannot enforce political investigations judicially it also does not need to tailor such inquiries to a rulemaking purpose. We should therefore expect that when Congress delegates its political investigations authority to the bureaucracy, bureaucrats would lack authority to legally enforce information demands to political officials while also being exempt from any requirement that their demands be narrowed to a particular regulatory purpose.

Consider that Inspectors General are tasked with investigating mismanagement within federal agencies and departments as well as empowered to use subpoenas to compel information from the private sector—especially government contractors. Consistent with expectations that direct political investigations by Congress are legally unenforceable, the Inspector General Act makes clear that Inspectors General may

> [R]equire by subpoena the production of all information, documents, reports, answers, records, accounts, papers, and other data in any medium (including electronically stored information), as well as any tangible thing and documentary evidence necessary in the performance of the functions assigned by this Act, which subpoenas, in the case of contumacy or refusal to obey, shall be enforceable by order of any appropriate United States district court: *Provided*, That **procedures other than subpoenas** shall be used by the Inspector General to obtain documents and information from Federal agencies[.][66]

The Inspector General Act reflects a separation of powers principle: because Congress cannot seek judicial redress for its direct investigations of the president and his copartisans, Congress could not circumvent such a restriction by creating legislative officers in the executive branch who could do indirectly what Congress is prohibited from doing directly.[67]

65 *Raines v. Byrd*, 521 U.S. 811, 818 (1997).

66 5 U.S.C. App. § 6(a)(4) (emphasis added).

67 *See e.g., Goland v. CIA*, 607 F.2d 339, 346 (D.C. Cir. 1978). *But* note that the Federal Housing Finance Authority Inspector General recently "served subpoenas on the FHFA Director[]" and obtained an "Order from a United State District Court[]" in clear violation of § 6(a) of the Inspector General Act. *See* FHFA OIG, *Report on Administrative Inquiry into Allegations of Misconduct by the FHFA Director* (Nov. 29, 2018) at 4, *available at* https://www.fhfaoig.gov/sites/default/files/OIG-2019-001.pdf#page=4.

Showing that Congress delegates its power to conduct political inquiries to the bureaucracy also helps address two explanatory holes in the general theory that Congress prefers to conduct oversight by establishing administrative procedures. First, if Congress prefers to conduct oversight through administrative procedures, then the general theory is strained by the fact that Congress still organizes a substantial part of its oversight capacity through a committee system.[68] The existence in Congress of permanent committees with dedicated oversight authority and oversight staff is difficult to justify as consistent with a congressional preference to rely on third parties to effectuate oversight. Second, and related, these committees have oversight agendas that are limited by jurisdictional rules. And that means that, for instance, two committees may have oversight over the Environmental Protection Agency yet different subagencies or programs within that agency, which means that interest groups risk pulling fire alarms that, e.g., the House Energy and Commerce Committee rejects as useful when the House Natural Resources Committee would have accepted the information as pivotal.[69] And interest groups cannot expect a spontaneous order where one committee's false negative is referred to another committee that might deem the information a true positive.[70]

But if we expect that Congress has its own bureaucratic agents tasked with providing jurisdictionally relevant information to the appropriate committees, then the expectation provides explanatory support for why

[68] *See* Joel Aberbach, *Keeping a Watchful Eye: The Politics of Congressional Oversight* 110 (1990).

[69] Sean Gailmard, *Discretion Rather Than Rules: Choice of Instruments to Control Bureaucratic Policy Making*, 17 Polit. Anal. 25–44 (2009) ("The commitment implicit in an action restriction could reflect, for example, the probability that the bureaucratic policy choice arouses the attention of the legislative principal. Because of gaps in legislative policy attention and imperfections in oversight, it is not unreasonable that this probability might be less than 1.... Understanding how this affects the legislature's choice of levers of control and how this interacts with, say, ex post oversight by the legislature updating its beliefs after bureau policy choice could also lead to interesting insights about bureaucratic discretion and accountability."); *accord* Sean Gailmard, *Expertise, Subversion, and Bureaucratic Discretion,* 18 J. L. Econ. Org. at 536–555 (2002) ("One direction to investigate is corruption. Delegation of decision making or administrative authority carries the danger that different decisions will be made, or will be made on different bases, than those desired by the delegator. The representation of subversion in this article is one way of capturing that.").

[70] *Id.*

Congress may rely on administrative procedures yet maintain a committee system with overlap concerning agencies within its jurisdiction.[71] While the passage of the Administrative Procedure Act (APA) in 1946 established *ex ante* administrative procedures,[72] the Legislative Reorganization Act (LRA) of 1946 can be interpreted to have established *ex post* administrative procedures. Scholars have generally not considered the relevance of both statutes to oversight and, in particular, oversight over bureaucratic investigations empowered through congressional delegation. Administrative procedures, established by laws like the LRA and the APA, ensure that both the committee system and congressional delegates of legislative power function in tandem to effectuate bureaucratic oversight.

These political expectations about administrative procedures informed their development. Congressman Walter, in describing the Administrative Procedure Act of 1946, stated, "[d]ay by day Congress takes account of the interests and desires of the people in framing legislation; and there is no reason why administrative agencies should not do so when they exercise legislative functions which Congress has delegated to them." Senator Pat McCarran called the APA "a bill of rights for the hundreds of thousands of Americans whose affairs are controlled or regulated in one way or another by agencies of the Federal Government. It is designed to provide guaranties of due process in administrative procedure." Political scientists who commented at the time on the 1946 LRA viewed the reform as a mechanism where Congress sought to empower itself with expertise and oversight tools to effectively cabin administrative discretion.[73] According to George Galloway, the Legislative Reorganization Act of 1946 intended to "bring about a three-way division of labor in the performance of the oversight function."[74] In this division of labor, the appropriations committees would exercise financial control before

[71] *See e.g.*, Kathleen Bawn, *Political Control Versus Expertise: Congressional Choices About Administrative Procedures*, 89 Am. Pol. Sci. Rev. (1995) at 62–73; Kathleen Bawn et al., *A Theory of Political Parties: Groups, Policy Demands and Nominations in American Politics*, 10 Perspect. Pol. (2012) at 571–597.

[72] McNollGast, *The Political Origins of the Administrative Procedure Act*, 15 J. L. Econ. & Org. (1999) at 180–217 (hereinafter McNollGast 1999).

[73] Ernest Griffith, Chapter VI, *Stokes Lectures*, delivered at New York University in April, 1951.

[74] George B. Galloway, *The Operation of the Legislative Reorganization Act of 1946*, 45 Am. Pol. Sci. Rev. (1951) at 59.

expenditures; the expenditures committees would review administrative structure and procedures; and the legislative (policy) committees would review the operation of substantive legislation and consider the need for statutory amendments.[75]

The 1946 LRA provides substantial hints for understanding how Congress delegates to the bureaucracy its power to engage in political probes, setting the groundwork for the creation of Inspectors General. The LRA established congressional standing committees and authorized them to exercise "continual watchfulness" over the executive branch, and the Legislative Reorganization Act of 1970, which created oversight-specific subcommittees, created the Congressional Research Service (CRS) within the Library of Congress, and further empowered the Government Accountability Office (GAO) as an investigative entity.[76] Both GAO, led by the presidentially appointed and Senate confirmed Comptroller General, and CRS are considered legislative agencies but the Supreme Court has found GAO to exercise executive powers and the CRS is housed within an agency headed by a presidential appointee: the Librarian of Congress.[77] While GAO's audit agenda is determined by legislative demands to study a matter or audit a program, its investigative agenda is set through requests from committee chairs.[78] In prior administrations, GAO has been utilized to investigate presidents and their copartisan appointees beyond mere programmatic audits.[79] The 1946

[75] *Id.* at 59. Of course, both the APA and the LRA were only possible because in November 1946 unified Democratic control of government broke when both houses flipped. The Democrats, foreseeing losses in the 80th Congress hedged against a full-fledged attack on the New Deal by agreeing to pass the APA and LRA and present the bills to President Truman for signature.

[76] Legislative Reorganization Act of 1946, P.L. 79-601 (codified at 2 U.S.C. § 31, hereinafter "1946 LRA"); Legislative Reorganization Act of 1970, P.L. 91-510 (hereinafter "1970 LRA"); *cf.* Walter Kravitz, *The Advent of the Modern Congress: The Legislative Reorganization Act of 1970*, 15 Leg. Stud. Qrtrly (1990) at 375–399.

[77] *See e.g.*, "GAO Access and Oversight Act of 2017", P.L. 115-3, § 2(c), amending 31 U.S.C. § 716 to empower "the Comptroller General [to] bring a civil action in the district court of the United States for the District of Columbia to require the head of the agency to produce a record[.]"

[78] 31 U.S.C. § 701, 707.

[79] *See e.g.*, U.S. Government Accountability Office, Decision, *Office of Management and Budget—Withholding of Ukraine Security Assistance*, No. B-331564 (Jan. 16, 2020) ("We consider a reluctance to provide a fulsome response to have constitutional significance. GAO's role … to provide information and legal analysis to Congress as it performs

LRA also established the Federal Regulation of Lobbying Act (the predecessor to the Lobbying Disclosure Act) and the Federal Tort Claims Act,[80] both of which established enforcement responsibilities on the presidentially supervised departments that were previously within Congress's investigative purview.

These reforms, in addition to the enlargement of powers given to GAO, presaged what I hypothesize typifies congressional delegation of its power to investigate the president and his copartisans: the creation of the departmental offices of Inspectors General.[81] Inspectors General, who are presidentially appointed, do not fit within the McNollGast model of "bureaucrats [who] have personal preferences which conflict with members of Congress and the president."[82] Inspector General disclosures to Congress do not involve "hearings, investigations, budget reviews, [or] legislative sanctions" by Congress.[83] Nor is the fire-alarm pulling by an Inspector General a "constituent complaint."[84]

The political kinship of the APA and the LRA has bred a statutory logic, for the APA amendments that provide public access to executive branch information (the Freedom of Information Act)[85] are codified in the same Title 5 of the United States Code that establishes the authority of the Inspectors General. While I am particularly interested in the section of Title 5 concerning the Inspector General Act, Title 5 represents the full arsenal of administrative procedures governing modern bureaucratic power—both procedures permitting affected parties to petition for judicial recourse as well as procedures regulating political appointees. Virtually every statute that delegates investigative authority to the bureaucracy and mandates a reporting requirement to Congress is codified in Title 5, including the Budget and Control Act of 1921 which

oversight of executive activity – is essential to ensuring respect for and allegiance to Congress's constitutional power of the purse.").

[80] 28 U.S.C. § 1346.

[81] Senate Government Operations report, *supra* note 54. The report defined congressional oversight as "a wide range of congressional efforts to review and control policy implementation by the regulatory agencies." Senate Government Operations report, *id.*, at 4.

[82] McNollGast 1987, *supra* note 5 in Chapter 3 at 247.

[83] *Id.* at 243.

[84] *Id.* at 250.

[85] 5 U.S.C. § 552(a)(4)(B).

created the Comptroller General who heads the Government Accountability Office,[86] the Hatch Act,[87] the Government Reports Act,[88] the creation of the Office of Special Counsel,[89] the Ethics in Government Act,[90] the Inspector General Act,[91] the Regulatory Flexibility Act[92] (and the Small Business Regulatory Enforcement Fairness Act), and the Congressional Review Act.[93] Additionally, all "whistleblower" laws empowering individuals to seek redress against the bureaucracy are codified in Title 5: in addition to the APA,[94] this includes FOIA,[95] the Privacy Act,[96] the Federal Advisory Committee Act,[97] the Whistleblower Protection Enhancement Act,[98] the Paperwork Reduction Act,[99] the Federal Records Act,[100] the Tucker Act,[101] and the False Claims Act.[102]

A major theoretical contribution of this book is to show that rather than Congress establishing administrative procedures anew in every policy

[86] 31 U.S.C. §§ 707, 717.

[87] 5 U.S.C. § 7321 *et seq.*

[88] 5 U.S.C. § 2954.

[89] 5 U.S.C. § 1212. Note also the sense in which these oversight delegates further delegate to whistleblowers. *See* Hatch Act Complaint Form, *available at* https://osc.gov/Documents/Resources/Forms/State,%20Local,%20%20and%20Nonprofit%20Complaint%20Form.pdf. The IRS empowers special interests to file complaints regarding other special interest groups violating their tax-exempt status. *See* IRS Form 13909, *available at* https://www.irs.gov/pub/irs-pdf/f13909.pdf. In neither case, do the organic statutes specifically authorize information collections of this sort. Both agencies engage in information collections to effectively administer statutes.

[90] 5 U.S.C. § Appx. Ethics in Government Act, § 101.

[91] 5 U.S.C. § Appx. Inspector General Act § 1.

[92] 5 U.S.C. § 601.

[93] 5 U.S.C. § 801.

[94] 5 U.S.C. § 551 *et seq.*

[95] 5 U.S.C. § 552.

[96] 5 U.S.C. § 552a.

[97] 5 U.S.C. § Appx. Federal Advisory Committee Act, § 1.

[98] 5 U.S.C. § 7211; 5 U.S.C. § 2302(a)(1).

[99] 44 U.S.C. § 3517(b) (reviewable by the APA).

[100] 44 U.S.C. § 2208.

[101] 28 U.S.C. § 1491. Note that the Tucker Act and the False Claims Act trace their authority to the adjudications by the eighteenth century Committee on Claims.

[102] 31 U.S.C. § 3729.

prescription enacted during a given session, Congress uses Title 5 of the United States Code to establish broad, policy-agnostic administrative procedures governing bureaucratic policymaking. Title 5 represents a set of statutes delegating oversight powers to citizens and bureaucratic fire chiefs which are ignored by scholars due to undertheorizing the administrative state's dynamics and Congress's oversight of its activities. Title 5 is itself a mirror of the twin goals of the 1946 LRA and APA: creating administrative procedures that enhance congressional control over the bureaucracy. Title 5 establishes procedures governing how the bureaucracy conducts investigations of businesses, writes rules to protect consumers, and adjudicates complaints claiming violations of rules by business; additionally, Title 5 establishes procedures empowering the bureaucracy to investigate the political officials and staff who nominally oversee the bureaucracy.

For some political scientists, congressional investigations are the means by which Congress oversees the bureaucracy. For other political scientists, Congress exercises oversight through administrative procedures. But neither model can explain what Title 5 makes evident: Congress delegates its investigative powers to the bureaucracy and establishes administrative procedures to monitor that delegation. What scholars measure as "police patrol" oversight—hearings, subpoenas, investigative reports—is *ex post* both delegation of investigative and rulemaking powers in agency enabling statutes and the administrative procedures of Title 5 empowering third parties (agency regulators, FOIA requesters, regulated companies, Inspectors General) to oversee implementation of those enabling statutes by the bureaucracy. And while law is helpful in explicating this model, the claim that Congress lacks an explicit constitutional or statutory right to monitor the bureaucracy misses the political forest for the legal trees. The bureaucracy itself was formed through congressional delegation of the legislative power of inquiry, reflecting that the principal–agent model for explaining congressional control of the bureaucracy provides persuasive reasons to reject legal scholars' reliance on a separation of powers formalism to explain the relationship between Congress and regulators.

Consistent with prior work, the picture presented so far supports the theory that administrative procedures arm congressional delegates with the ability to ensure the bureaucracy does not drift from congressional intent concerning the regulatory objectives of statutes implemented by the agencies. But if the model suggested here is to be convincing, it must explain why Congress does anything indicative of direct oversight when the nature of administrative procedures is to curb agency drift without active congressional intervention. The contention is that if the model is accurate, then the work of oversight committees and their staff cannot be explained or must, alternatively, be motivated not by concerns about policy drift but out of the political interest of members of Congress to most efficiently obtain and disclose information to help or hurt the presidential administration electorally.

2 The Legal Dynamics of Political Oversight

2.1 *The Supreme Court's Recognition of Bureaucratic Investigations as Legislative, Not Executive, Powers*

If legislative power includes ancillary investigative powers, and oversight is responsive to delegation of legislative power, the concept of oversight must account for congressional delegations to the bureaucracy of investigative powers over political officials and the private sphere. The Supreme Court, just seven years after the creation of the Interstate Commerce Commission (ICC), recognized the ICC as a "tribunal" of Congress whose authority to investigate the private sphere was a power Congress exercised "as a basis for intelligent legislation" and something "within legislative cognizance."[103] By 1912, congressional delegation to the administrative state was easily managed judicially, for the administrative state was characterized by investigative and adjudicative powers, which the Supreme Court distinguished from "regulation," which was still the purview of direct action by Congress.[104] The Supreme Court, in 1928, held that it was permissible for Congress to "use executive officers in the application and enforcement of a policy declared in law by Congress, and authorize such officers in the application of the Congressional declaration to enforce it by regulation equivalent to law."[105] Administrative enforcement of policy through a rule or order was distinguished in kind from

[103] *ICC v. Brimson*, 154 U.S. 447, 474–477 (1894).

[104] *Interstate Commerce Comm'n v. Goodrich Transit Co.*, 224 U.S. 194, 211 (1912).

[105] *J. W. Hampton, Jr., & Co. v. United States*, 276 U.S. 394, 409 (1928); *accord. Marshall Field & Co. v. Clark*, 143 U.S. 649, 693 (1892) ("enforcement of the policy established by Congress").

constitutional enforcement of a law or regulation by executive officers before the judiciary.[106]

The Supreme Court's tenuous distinction between regulation-as-policy enforcement and executive action-as-law enforcement ultimately collapsed, for any attempt to ensure the executive branch acted with one voice, namely the president, ended with *Humphrey's Executor*.[107] In its 1935 *Humphrey's Executor* decision, the Supreme Court determined that the Federal Trade Commission, the next administrative creation after the ICC, was "an administrative body created by Congress to carry into effect legislative policies embodied in the statute in accordance with the legislative standard therein prescribed, and to perform other specified duties as a legislative or as a judicial aid."[108]

And by 1946, the Supreme Court recognized administrative subpoena powers—those used to enforce administrative investigations—to be "incidental to both [Congress's] general legislative and its investigative powers" under the "'necessary and proper' clause."[109] Prior to 1935, the Supreme Court recognized executive branch rules and orders to be law enforcement subject to the president's discretion.[110] Once the Supreme Court recognized that agencies and commissions could be independent from presidential supervision, regulation could no longer be understood

[106] *Marshall Field & Co. v. Clark*, 143 U.S. 649, 693 (1892).

[107] Supreme Court scholars argue that *Humphrey's* has been effectively overturned. *See e.g., Bowsher v. Synar*, 478 U.S. 714, 733 (1986) ("Interpreting a law enacted by Congress to implement the legislative mandate is the very essence of 'execution' of the law").

[108] *Humphrey's Ex'r v. U.S.*, 295 U.S. 602, 628 (1935). The *Humphrey's* Court unfortunately conceived of agency adjudications as "quasi-judicial" when, as shown in Part I, Congress engaged in adjudications for the purpose of promulgating private relief bills—a power delegated to the bureaucracy as adjudication. This is of course why the Court of Federal Claims is a legislative court—its adjudications are of claims for private relief and its affirmative orders function as the promulgation of private relief bills directing the U.S. Treasury to pay money to a petitioner.

[109] *Okla. Press Pub. Co. v. Walling*, 327 U.S. 186, 201, 214 (1946).

[110] *Marshall Field*, supra note 105 at 694–695 (referencing *Cincinnati, Wilmington & Co. Railroad v. Commissioners*, 1 Ohio St. 88 ("'The true distinction,' as Judge Ranney speaking for the Supreme Court of Ohio has well said, 'is between the delegation of power to make the law, which necessarily involves a discretion as to what it shall be, and conferring authority or discretion as to its execution, to be exercised under and in pursuance of the law. The first cannot be done; to the latter no valid objection can be made.'")).

as within presidential discretion.[111] Instead, Congress could delegate "decisionmaking authority upon agencies" by "lay[ing] down by legislative act an intelligible principle to which the person or body authorized to act is directed to conform."[112]

2.2 *Congressional Oversight of the Bureaucracy as an Implied Power Arising from Delegation*

Current scholarship identifies oversight of the bureaucracy, as opposed to regulatory investigations or public education-oriented scrutiny of political officials, as an institution arising as the result of Congress delegating its rulemaking power, albeit historically subsequent to its delegation of investigative and adjudicative powers,[113] to "quasi-legislative" agencies[114] charged with administering statutes.[115]

The legal distinction between rulemaking and adjudication as what legislative agencies, as opposed to law enforcement (executive) departments, do is codified in the Administrative Procedure Act.[116] The Legislative Reorganization Act of 1946, which established a set of standing committees in the House and Senate to "exercise continuous watchfulness over administration," was authored by the same congressional membership that wrote the Administrative Procedure Act as a set of governing rules over the administrative agencies that were delegated powers by Congress.[117]

[111] Cox & McCubbins, *supra* note 21 in Chapter 3; David Lewis & Jennifer Selin, *Political Control and the Forms of Agency Independence*, 83 George Wash. L. Rev. (2015) at 1487–1516.

[112] *Whitman v. Am. Trucking Ass'ns*, 531 U.S. 457, 472 (U.S. 2001) (citing *J. W. Hampton, Jr., & Co.* v. *United States*, 276 U.S. 394, 409 (1928)).

[113] *Ex parte Bakelite Corp.*, 279 U.S. 438, 452–453 (1929). The 1929 Supreme Court considered the Court of Claims as a delegation of Congress's "examination and determination" powers over private claims.

[114] *Humphrey's Ex'r*, *supra* note 37 at 624.

[115] Humphrey's clarifies the distinction between "political" or "executive" powers and the "quasi-judicial and quasi-legislative" powers of administrative agencies. *Id.*

[116] 5 U.S.C. § 551.

[117] Legislative Reorganization Act of 1946 (60 Stat. 812).

Political scientists are generally unified in their view that oversight involves political control of the bureaucracy.[118] Yet legal scholars conceive of oversight as Congress's power to investigate for the purposes of legislating intelligibly.[119] While such a doctrine justifies congressional investigations of the private sphere, the cases informing the doctrine exclude attempts to enforce inquiries against the bureaucracy or political officials. This presents a doctrinal problem, for the historical discussion reveals that under the Constitution, Congress may enforce its investigative inquiries of the private sector under the need to serve its legislative function (derived from the "Necessary and Proper" clause) and Congress may enforce its investigations against political appointees through removal (derived from the impeachment clause). But which constitutional provision justifies congressional monitoring of bureaucratic policymaking? Asked another way, and as informed by Epstein and O'Halloran's examination of the nondelegation doctrine,[120] if Congress is prohibited from delegating policymaking authority to the bureaucracy, then on what basis could Congress exercise oversight of the bureaucracy?

Oversight is the authority to monitor bureaucratic implementation of delegated power.[121] Its authority is prudential, not constitutional: that the bureaucracy exercises legislative power requires Congress to monitor how its agents exercise *its* authority and is "incident to the distribution of the governmental powers among three departments[.]"[122] While the president's authority is rooted in the Constitution, "an agency literally has no power to act ... unless and until Congress confers power upon it".[123] In Congress's own words, "oversight of regulatory agencies, of course,

[118] David Epstein & Sharyn O'Halloran, *The Nondelegation Doctrine and the Separation of Powers: A Political Science Approach*, 20 Cardozo L. Rev. 947, n. 26–37 (1999) (citing numerous political science studies) [hereinafter "Epstein & O'Halloran (1999b)"].

[119] "[T]here's no [constitutional] provision expressly investing either house with power to make investigations and exact testimony, to the end that it may exercise its legislative function advisedly and effectively." *McGrain v. Daugherty*, 273 U.S. 135, 161 (1927).

[120] Epstein & O'Halloran (1999b), *supra* note 118.

[121] Lisa Schultz Bressman, Schechter Poultry *at the Millennium: A Delegation Doctrine for the Administrative State*, 109 Yale L.J. 1399, 1416 (2000). (discussing the "new delegation doctrine" where Congress writes administrative procedures to control delegated policymaking).

[122] *Myers v. United States*, 272 U.S. 52, 293 (1926) (Brandeis, J., dissenting).

[123] *Louisiana Public Service Commission v. FCC*, 476 U.S. 355, 374 (1986).

did not begin until after the agencies themselves were created, almost 100 years later."[124]

The Legislative Reorganization Act provides support for justifying oversight of bureaucratic policymaking under the same authority Congress has to delegate legislative powers to committees—the "rules of proceedings" clause of Article I.[125] "Congress' authority to investigate includes the authority to compel the production of information by issuing subpoenas, a power the House has delegated to its committees pursuant to its Constitutional authority to 'determine the Rules of its Proceedings.'"[126] The only statute to address the congressional oversight power, the 1946 LRA,[127] grounded Congress's power to "exercise continuous watchfulness of the execution by the administrative agencies concerned of any laws[,]"[128] in the "rule-making power of the Senate and the House of Representatives[.]"[129]

Alternatively, it is often stated that the power to conduct oversight originates from Congress's "power of the purse."[130] The Supreme Court has acknowledged that Article I, Clause 7 of the U.S. Constitution states that "a regular Statement and Account of the Receipts and Expenditures of all public Money shall be published from time to time" and that therefore "Congress has a plenary power to exact any reporting or accounting it considers appropriate in the public interest."[131] The Supreme Court, however, has described the notion of a congressional power of "general supervision of the operations of government" as "amorphous."[132] Whether based upon rules of proceedings or the power of the purse, direct congressional oversight lacks an enforceable remedy because the

[124] Senate Government Operations report, *supra* note 54 at 8.

[125] Section 101 of the Legislative Reorganization Act of 1946 governs the "Rule-making power of the Senate and House". P.L. 79-601 § 101 (hereinafter Legislative Reorganization Act of 1946).

[126] U.S. House of Representatives, Permanent Select Committee on Intelligence, *The Trump-Ukraine Impeachment Inquiry Report*, *available at* https://intelligence.house.gov/report/.

[127] LRA *supra* note 76.

[128] *Id.* at § 136.

[129] *Id.* at § 101.

[130] *United States v. Richardson*, 418 U.S. 166 (1974).

[131] *Id.* at 178, note 11.

[132] *Id.* at 192 (Powell, J. concurring).

Supreme Court has held that Congress cannot bind an individual or entity outside the Congress with its internal procedures.[133] By establishing procedures of judicial review governing compliance with its delegations of authority, Congress is able to do indirectly what it would be prohibited from doing directly.[134]

Legal scholars have not adopted this understanding of delegation and oversight.[135] This is in large part due to the nondelegation doctrine and unitary executive views requiring presidential supervision of the bureaucracy, as introduced in Part I and discussed more fully in the next section.

2.3 The Institutional Response to the Legislative Bureaucracy: Unitary Executive Theory, Nondelegation Doctrine, and "Accommodation"

The notion among political scientists that Congress can exercise control over the bureaucracy immediately threatens the legal doctrine that Congress cannot permissibly vest its legislative power in the executive branch. The "Necessary and Proper" Clause justified Congress's power to investigate the private sphere as well as its authority to delegate that power to the bureaucracy. And it would logically justify the monitoring of such delegation. But not for our current legal institutions. The legal doctrine supporting oversight derives from the begrudging acceptance of bureaucratic policymaking best reflected in Justice White's dissent in *Bowsher v. Synar*:

> [The Supreme Court has recognized that] it is within the power of Congress under the "Necessary and Proper" Clause, Art. I, § 8, to vest authority that falls within the Court's definition of executive power in

[133] *Yellin v. United States*, 374 U.S. 109, 143 (1963) ("the manner in which a house or committee of Congress chooses to run its business ordinarily raises no justiciable controversy"); *accord. INS v. Chadha*, 462 U.S. 919, 952 (1983).

[134] *Id.* ("when the application or construction of a rule directly affects persons other than members of the house, 'the question presented is of necessity a judicial one'") (citing *United States v. Smith*, 286 U.S. 6, 33; *Christoffel* v. *United States*, 338 U.S. 84).

[135] Jack M. Beermann, *Congressional Administration*, 43 San Diego L. Rev. 61, 64–65 (2006); Mark Seidenfeld, *The Psychology of Accountability and Political Review of Agency Rules*, 51 Duke L. J. 1059 (2001). Jonathan R. Macey, *Organizational Design and Political Control of Administrative Agencies*, 8 J. L. Econ. & Org. 93 (1992).

> officers who are not subject to removal at will by the president and are therefore not under the president's direct control. *See, e.g., Humphrey's Executor v. United States*, 295 U.S. 602 (1935); *Wiener v. United States*, 357 U.S. 349 (1958). In an earlier day, in which simpler notions of the role of government in society prevailed, it was perhaps plausible to insist that all "executive" officers be subject to an unqualified Presidential removal power, *see Myers v. United States*, 272 U.S. 52 (1926); but with the advent and triumph of the administrative state and the accompanying multiplication of the tasks undertaken by the Federal Government, the Court has been virtually compelled to recognize that Congress may reasonably deem it "necessary and proper" to vest some among the broad new array of governmental functions in officers who are free from the partisanship that may be expected of agents wholly dependent upon the president.[136]

The Department of Justice's Office of Legal Counsel, whose opinions bind the president and the bureaucracy, has challenged "the continuing validity of *Humphrey's Executor.*"[137] By rejecting the continuing validity of *Humphrey's Executor*, the bureaucracy can deny that bureaucratic policymaking exists. Instead, all bureaucratic activity, including rulemaking and adjudication, are law enforcement activities subject to the supervision of the president, as chief executive.

Both the executive branch and Congress have interpreted the investigative authority Congress has over the private sphere as justifying "oversight"—Congress's ability to control bureaucratic policymaking. To illustrate this move, the Office of Legal Counsel at the U.S. Department of Justice conflates Congress's "authority to make official inquiries into and to conduct investigations of executive branch programs and activities" with "the implicit authority of each house of Congress to gather information in aid of its legislative function."[138]

Just like the Office of Legal Counsel (OLC) has rejected the validity of presidentially insulated agencies exercising legislative powers, OLC has also rejected the executive branch's position, from Washington through Nixon, that responding to congressional oversight requests is within the

[136] *Bowsher v. Synar*, 478 U.S. 714, 760–762 (1986).

[137] *Applicability of Executive Privilege to the Recommendations of Independent Agencies Regarding Presidential Approval or Veto of Legislation*, 10 O.L.C. Op. 176, 178 (Dec. 22, 1986) (citing footnote 3 of *Bowsher v. Synar*, 478 U.S. 714, 761 (1986)).

[138] *Authority of Individual Members of Congress to Conduct Oversight of the executive branch*, 41 O.L.C. Op. at 1 (May 1, 2017) (hereinafter May 1, 2017 OLC Opinion).

executive branch's discretion as to whether compliance would advance the public interest. Once Congress prevailed in the federal courts concerning its requests for information from the Nixon White House,[139] and the Supreme Court concluded that executive privilege was not absolute,[140] the executive branch moved to concede the legality of oversight in Congress's investigative powers *writ large* while arguing that the activities and communications of the president, his advisers, and high-level executive branch officials are entitled to a presumption of confidentiality.

Thus rather than rely on the noticeable absence of constitutional text, the federal government and the courts have determined that "oversight" is a power "so far incidental to the legislative function as to be implied."[141] Because of the courts' refusal to recognize the constitutional legitimacy of congressional delegation, Congress, the executive branch, and the federal courts have justified congressional investigations of the bureaucracy under the holdings established through disputes between Congress and individuals, where oversight is justified whenever it is for a legitimate legislative purpose.[142] This compromise has been

139 *Senate Select Committee on Presidential Campaign Activities v. Nixon*, 498 F.2d 725 (D.C. Cir. 1974).

140 *United States v. Nixon*, 418 U.S. 683, 693 (1974).

141 *McGrain*, supra note 119.

142 *McGrain v. Daugherty*, 273 U.S. 135, 154 (1927); *U.S. v. Bryan*, 72 F. Supp. 58, 61 (D.C. Cir. 1947) ("If the subject under scrutiny may have any possible relevancy and materiality, no matter how remote, to some possible legislation, it is within the power of the Congress to investigate the matter. Moreover, the relevancy and the materiality of the subject matter must be presumed."); *Barsky v. U.S.*, 167 F.2d 241, 250 (D.C. Cir. 1948) ("The courts have no authority to speak or act upon the conduct by the legislative branch of its own business, so long as the bounds of power and pertinency are not exceeded"); *McGrain v. Daugherty*, 273 U.S. 135, 175 (1927) ("[a] legislative body cannot legislate wisely or effectively in the absence of information respecting the conditions which the legislation is intended to affect or change."); *accord Anderson v. Dunn*, 6 Wheat. 204 (1821); *United States v. Rumely*, 345 U.S. 41, 46 (1953); *Watkins v. United States*, 354 U.S. 178, 187 (1957) (curtailing House Un-American Activities Committee inquiries into witnesses' personal beliefs, although dictum affirmed that Congress's "broad [power] ... to conduct investigations is inherent in the legislative process"); *Tenney v. Brandhove*, 341 U.S. 367, 377–378 (U.S. 1951) ("To find that a committee's investigation has exceeded the bounds of legislative power it must be obvious that there was a usurpation of functions exclusively vested in the Judiciary or the Executive."); *Tenney*, 341 U.S. at 377 ("Investigations, whether by standing or special committees, are an established part of representative government."); *Barenblatt v. United States*, 360 U.S. 109, 111 (1959) ("The scope of the [congressional] power of inquiry ... is as penetrating and far-reaching

counterbalanced by the OLC's position that the Constitution creates a judicially rebuttable presumption of the confidentiality of executive branch communications.[143]

While OLC argues "disputes over congressional demands for information from the executive branch are inherently political, and the historical practice has been to resolve such questions in the political arena,"[144] it has favored a doctrine where each branch is under an "implicit constitutional mandate to seek optimal accommodation" with the other under a "spirit of dynamic compromise."[145]

This accommodation doctrine is aimed at avoiding judicial review of interbranch disputes.[146] The political motivations behind mutating the complex legal distinctions between Congress's non-judicially enforceable oversight of the bureaucracy and Congress's judicially enforceable investigative power informs the relevant political science literature where scholars have referred to the characteristics of congressional oversight, i.e., position-taking publicity with *ex post* monitoring, as "two purposes, by-products of American constitutional design[.]"[147]

The implication of these legal moves for American politics is that it presumes that congressional capacity for oversight is enhanced through

as the potential power to enact and appropriate, [subject to the limitation that] Congress may only investigate into those areas in which it may potentially legislate or appropriate."); *Eastland v. U.S. Servicemen's Fund*, 421 U.S. 491, 503–507 (1975) (members of Congress cannot be sued for alleged constitutional violations stemming from issuing subpoenas to individuals to appear before a congressional committee because the Constitution's Speech and Debate Clause encompasses legislators' subpoena powers); *id.* at 504 ("The power to investigate and to do so through compulsory process plainly falls within [the definition of legislative activity] ... "Issuance of subpoenas ... has long been held to be a legitimate use by Congress of its power to investigate."); *Nixon v. Adm'r of Gen. Servs.*, 433 U.S. 425, 453 (1977) (stating Congress may act to preserve White House documents related to President Nixon's resignation, executive privilege notwithstanding, since the possibility that such documents could be relevant to future legislation places their preservation within the scope of Congress's investigative power).

143 *Testimonial Immunity Before Congress of the Former Counsel to the President*, 41 Op. O.L.C. 1, 12 (May 20, 2019).

144 *Id.*

145 *Id.* at 17.

146 *United States v. American Tel. & Tel. Co.*, 551 F.2d 384, 390 (D.C. Cir. 1976) (hereinafter "AT&T 1"); *United States v. AT&T*, 567 F.2d 121, 127 (D.C. Cir. 1977) (hereinafter "AT&T 2").

147 Parker and Dull (2013), *supra* note 43 in Chapter 3.

investigations of the administrative state tailored to some regulatory purpose. The theoretical discussion in Part I has sought to clarify the doctrinal grounds for distinguishing between oversight and other legislative inquiries. The next chapter identifies the empirical expectation that Congress best controls the bureaucracy when it shifts resources away from direct monitoring toward administrative procedures attached to its legislative delegations. Chapter 4 models those expectations.

CHAPTER 3

Congressional Delegation of Its Power to Monitor Policy Implementation

In American politics, delegation occurs when Congress legislatively empowers agencies to administer policies with the force of law.[1] Delegation is of scholarly interest because of the expectation that elected officials will be motivated to ensure agencies exercising delegated authority act consistently with political preferences.[2] This need to monitor or control agency implementation of legislative mandates is described by scholars as "oversight."[3] We should therefore expect that oversight and delegation are interrelated.[4]

[1] Jason Webb Yackee & Susan Webb Yackee, *From Legislation to Regulation: An Empirical Examination of Agency Responsiveness to Congressional Delegations of Regulatory Authority*, 68 Admin. L. Rev. 395, 396 (2016) (hereinafter "Yackee & Yackee").

[2] Kenneth A. Shepsle, *Bureaucratic Drift, Coalitional Drift, and Time Consistency: A Comment on Macey*, 8 J. L. Econ. & Org. 111, 113–115 (1992).

[3] John D. Huber & Charles R. Shipan, *Deliberate Discretion? The Institutional Foundations of Bureaucratic Autonomy*, at 26 (2002); Robert McGrath, *Congressional Oversight Hearings and Policy Control*, 38 Leg. Stud. Qrtrly (2013) at 349–376.

[4] David Epstein & Sharyn O'Halloran, *A Theory of Strategic Oversight: Congress, Lobbyists, and the Bureaucracy*, 11 J. L. Econ. & Org. (1995) at 227–255; John D. Huber & Charles R. Shipan, *Deliberate Discretion? The Institutional Foundations of Bureaucratic Autonomy* (2002); Sean Gailmard, *Expertise, Subversion, and Bureaucratic Discretion*, 18 J. L. Econ. & Org. (2002) at 536–555.

D. Z. Epstein, *The Investigative State: Regulatory Oversight in the United States*, https://doi.org/10.1007/978-3-031-38461-5_3

When it comes to oversight of the bureaucracy, political scientists have argued that contrary to the popular image of Congress aggressively overseeing executive branch agencies through headline-grabbing hearings and intensive prosecution-like investigations, Congress's preferred method of oversight is regulating the regulators—writing administrative procedures into law—that insure against policy drift by the agency.[5] This is not to say that congressional hearings and investigations of the executive branch do not occur. But brick-and-mortar oversight, unlike procedural monitoring, may be motivated by electoral incentives of members,[6] rather than institutional incentives of policy control, and may focus on the president and his copartisans (the "administration") rather than the policymaking bureaucracy.[7] For those scholars who specify administrative procedures as a key mechanism for oversight, investigative activity, and hearings by Congress are informed by evidence of bureaucratic drift from ideal policy outcomes first discovered by third parties legislatively empowered to expose procedural violations.

The following thematic issues motivate my book: Because scholars define oversight as the political monitoring of the bureaucracy, their theories generally exclude congressional inquiries and hearings targeted at the private sector or toward the president and his appointees from the scope of legislative power and therefore from the sorts of regulatory activities, delegated by Congress, that would be subject to oversight.[8] Unlike the

[5] Matthew McCubbins & Thomas Schwartz, *Congressional Oversight Overlooked: Police Patrols versus Fire Alarms*, 28 Am. J. Pol. Sci. at 165–179 (1984). Matthew McCubbins, Roger Noll, & Barry Weingast, *Administrative Procedures as Instruments of Political Control*, 3 J. L. Econ. & Org. at 243–277 (1987) (hereinafter "McNollGast 1987"); *see also* Arthur Lupia & Mathew D. McCubbins, *Designing Bureaucratic Accountability*, 57 Law & Contemp. Prob. 91 (1994); Mathew D. McCubbins, Roger Noll, & Barry Weingast, *Structure and Process, Politics and Policy: Administrative Arrangements and the Political Control of Agencies*, 75 Va. L. Rev. 431, 440–444 (1989) (hereinafter "McNollGast 1989").

[6] Lisa Schultz Bressman, *Procedures as Politics in Administrative Law*, 107 Colum. L. Rev. 1749, 1751 (2007) ("legal scholars have overlooked the possibility that administrative law doctrine may serve a political function by setting rules for how agencies operate").

[7] *See e.g.*, Alexander Bolton & Sharece Thrower, *Checks in the Balance: Legislative Capacity and the Dynamics of Executive Power* (2021) at 21 (evaluating unilateral action by "presidents and other chief executives").

[8] David Epstein & Sharyn O'Halloran, *Delegating Powers: A Transaction Cost Politics Approach to Policy Making Under Separate Powers*, 5 (1999) (the "modern administrative state" results from "the delegation of broad decision-making authority to a professional

federal administrative state, neither the president nor the private sector is created by, nor granted the power to regulate through, congressional delegation.[9] Congressional delegation is the condition precedent for both the existence and empowerment of the federal bureaucracy. The problem with excluding congressional investigations of the private sphere and the administration from the concept of oversight is that Congress uses its oversight committees to investigate the president as well as the private sphere.[10] Further, and as relevant to scholars, while the model connecting oversight to delegation may have significant explanatory power, the model may be limited in characterizing the scope of delegation due to how it understands legislative power, delegation, and bureaucratic policymaking.

1 The Law of Delegation and the Politics of Oversight

In Chapter 2, I analyzed the relevant political science and legal literatures to examine the possibility that Congress delegates its investigative powers to the bureaucracy and establishes administrative procedures to monitor such delegation. In this chapter, I extend that analysis into a framework from which we could empirically examine whether the expectation in the literature that Congress prefers to delegate its authority to the bureaucracy and then monitor bureaucratic policymaking through administrative procedures holds true when Congress delegates its investigative powers over the private sector and political officials to the bureaucracy. Observing a relationship between congressional oversight activities and the establishment of administrative procedures governing administrative investigations would reflect an electoral connection between delegation and oversight.

civil service[.]") (hereinafter "Epstein & O'Halloran 1999a"). Note also that Kriner & Schickler (2014), *infra*, distinguish between "misconduct investigations" targeting the president and his cabinet and "oversight."

[9] Yackee & Yackee, *supra* note 1 at 400 (further defining legislative power as rulemaking).

[10] Note that although considered an established doctrine among public law scholars that "oversight" and "legislation" are intertwined, for Congress, "[a] distinction can be made between legislative and oversight jurisdiction. Legislative jurisdiction describes the authority of a committee to receive and report measures to the House. Oversight jurisdiction refers to a committee's ability to review matters within its purview, for instance by conducting hearings and investigations." Mark J. Oleszek, *Committee Jurisdiction and Referral in the House*, CRS Report for Congress No. R46251 (Mar. 4, 2020) at 5.

This chapter focuses on developing the hypotheses I seek to test in the empirical chapter (Chapter 4).

What is the significance of Congress delegating its investigative powers to the bureaucracy for our understanding of congressional oversight and executive branch politics? The book's revised picture of oversight would have obvious implications for the understanding of American politics. First, it would clarify that bureaucratic policymaking (regulation) includes investigations of the private sector and of political officials in addition to the issuing of rules.[11] Second, those agency investigations of the private sector or political officials which derive from the bureaucracy's policymaking authority can be distinguished from executive branch activities to enforce, through the courts, policies determined through rulemaking or adjudication or fall within the law enforcement discretion of the president. Third, by viewing bureaucratic investigations and adjudications as legislative in nature, the book supports a legal theory that the existence of administrative procedures, rather than "intelligible principles" attached to authorizations by Congress, prevents the unlawful vesting of the legislative power outside of Congress. Administrative procedures,[12] rather than legislative standards, permit congressional control over "bureaucrats [who] have personal preferences which conflict with members of Congress and the president."[13]

Understanding certain agency action as policymaking versus law enforcement offers substantial clarity in both the American politics and administrative law literatures. Administrative law doctrine supposes that agencies have the discretion to choose to regulate either through promulgating laws that apply to an entire class (rulemaking) or issuing judgments that apply to individuals (adjudication). But regulatory scholars do not have a precise model for identifying when that binary choice arises or ends in the bureaucratic policy process. Scholars might suggest that litigation of an agency complaint before the Administrative Law Judge (ALJ) is certainly adjudication and possibly law enforcement. Likewise, judicial enforcement of a commission's decision to affirm or reverse an ALJ decision is certainly law enforcement and possibly adjudication. Are

[11] It is a pervasive rule of administrative law that agencies act *either* through rulemaking or adjudication. *SEC v. Chenery Corp.* (Chenery II), 332 U.S. 194, 203 (1947).

[12] McNollGast 1987, *supra* note 5 at 250.

[13] *Id.* at 247.

agency investigations of multiple regulated parties prior to the issuance of a complaint clearly adjudications? What if those pre-complaint investigations lead to the promulgation of a notice of proposed rulemaking or a complaint before a commission targeted to only one of several companies subject to investigation? Adopting legal models that apply to congressional activities and applying them to the bureaucracy helps classify agency discretion in procedural terms. While a complaint before an ALJ involves adjudication by the agency or a notice of proposed rulemaking involves rulemaking, an investigation that takes place before either action and which affects the private sector must always be for a rulemaking purpose. When the Select Committee on Commerce wrote proposed public laws while the Committee on Claims adjudicated private disputes for the purpose of drafting private bills, the investigative work of the Interstate Commerce Commission was justified by its ability to inform congressional rule-writing. Bureaucratic public law ends with final rules; bureaucratic private bill adjudications end with final orders; in the legislative process, final rules and orders are enforced only by the president whereas congressional activities, including investigations, that occur prior to the decision-making process leading to a final rule or order are rulemakings.

When the process is delegated to the bureaucracy, these analytic metes and bounds are no different. The APA defines "rule making" as the "agency process for formulating, amending, or repealing a rule."[14] Given the context that Congress can either promulgate private or public rules, the APA defines "rule" as "the whole or a part of an agency statement of **general** or **particular** applicability and future effect designed to implement, interpret, or prescribe law or policy[.]"[15] The theory of the unitary executive, however, deems no activities of the bureaucracy, itself composed of executive branch agencies, to be legislative in nature. All discretionary executive branch activity is analytically within the president's "take care" powers and thus constitutes law enforcement.

Within the broader political science literature, showing that Congress relies upon administrative procedures to monitor bureaucratic investigations and adjudications challenges those legal doctrines that describe

[14] 5 U.S.C. § 551(5).

[15] 5 U.S.C. § 551(4) (emphasis added).

such bureaucratic activities not as policymaking but as law enforcement. Administrative procedures that stack the deck for politically favored constituencies[16] should govern the range of regulatory activity, beyond final orders or rules, including investigative activities.[17] If oversight relates to delegation and the bureaucracy can regulate through legislative rulemaking and legislative investigations as delegated by Congress, then empirical support for these expectations would buttress the formal definition of oversight as limited to monitoring the bureaucracy.

As such, direct congressional investigations of the private sector or the presidential administration would be outside the political model of oversight. And these political models ought to inform the legal doctrines that bind political institutions. Constitutional justifications for legislative investigations of businesses or political activities, via the necessary and proper clause or the impeachment power, respectively, would mean that those activities are outside the scope of oversight. Oversight is limited to monitoring of the bureaucracy even when that bureaucracy does more than regulate through rules by investigating the private sector and political officials. For scholars of political science, the ability to distinguish between those legislative inquiries within the model of oversight and those outside it would support a strong implication that formal models of "congressional oversight" can be cabined within the doctrines of administrative law, for the institution of oversight would be governed by legal rules in the form of administrative procedures.[18] The range of bureaucratic activity subject to congressional oversight is *broader* than what scholars have traditionally modeled. At the same time, the concept that oversight is limited to the bureaucracy. Whenever Congress investigates non-bureaucratic targets directly, those investigations are not oversight. Under the framework constructed by McCubbins & Schwartz, we should rarely observe direct investigative activities of political officials or the private sector by Congress.

[16] *Id.* at 261 ("by controlling the details of procedures and participation, *political actors stack the deck in favor of constituents who are the intended beneficiaries of the bargain struck by the coalition which created the agency*").

[17] *Id.* at 256 ("the principal design criterion for an administrative process is likely to be procedural fairness").

[18] Jennifer Selin & Caylie Milazzo, *The Law*: "*If Men Were Angels*": *The Legal Dynamics of Overseeing the Executive Branch*, 51 Pres. Stud. Qrtl'y (2021) at 1–24.

Understanding oversight as monitoring bureaucratic investigations of officials and the private sector, in addition to monitoring bureaucratic rules and orders, presents a flexible explanatory framework for understanding legislative and executive institutions. To assess whether divided government increases congressional oversight,[19] we would look to distinguish between congressional hearings based on committee investigations of the bureaucracy from those hearings focused on the private sector or the discretionary activities of the administration. That divided government may lead to more inquiries toward the president and his copartisans may evidence legislative capacity but would not evidence expanded congressional oversight, if oversight is tied to the monitoring of delegated power.[20] Scholarly findings that investigations and hearings targeted to the administration are motivated by electoral interests,[21] or ideological interests,[22] does not mean that hearings concerning bureaucratic programs and operations are similarly motivated. The theory of oversight presented here merits distinguishing between whether Congress relies on police-patrol[23] procedures for investigating the administration or the private sector but "fire-alarm"[24] procedures for investigating the bureaucracy. And if the constitutional basis for oversight of the bureaucracy is distinct from impeachment power-justified probes into a presidential administration or necessary and proper clause-justified probes of the private sector, the model presented here has implications for when Congress should rely on the political process, rather than the courts, to resolve interbranch disputes.

[19] Douglas Kriner & Liam Schwartz, *Divided Government and Congressional Investigations*, 33 Leg. Stud. Qrtly (2008) at 298 (hereinafter "Kriner & Schwartz").

[20] Sean Gailmard, *Discretion Rather Than Rules: Choice of Instruments to Control Bureaucratic Policy Making*, 17 Pol. Anal. (2009).

[21] Kriner & Schwartz, *supra* note 19 at 299 ("hounding opposition-party officials under divided government carries the promise of electoral benefits") (relying on Aldrich 1995; Cox & McCubbins 1993; Kiewiet & McCubbins 1991).

[22] Epstein & O'Halloran (1999a), *supra* note 8.

[23] Joel Aberbach, *Keeping a Watchful Eye: The Politics of Congressional Oversight* (1990).

[24] Mathew McCubbins & Thomas Schwartz, *Congressional Oversight Overlooked: Police Patrols vs. Fire Alarms*, 28 Am. J. of Pol. Sci. (1984) at 165–179.

In this chapter, I outline my expectations concerning a predicted relationship between delegation of investigative powers and congressional policymaking capacity.

2 Effects of Investigative Delegations on Congressional Oversight

Through congressional delegation of legislative power to the bureaucracy, the bureaucracy is able to regulate the private sector through investigations that lead to binding rules and orders. Delegation also permits the bureaucracy to regulate political officials through investigations and findings by officials like the Special Counsel, the various Inspectors General, and the Comptroller General. While interest groups representing the private sector can go public about their concerns with regulatory policy by going to the media and the media can track and comment upon policy decisions by regulators or investigative findings by IGs, the incentive for interest groups to seek to set the direct, public oversight agenda of Congress is informed by the ability of members of Congress, particularly those with committee oversight authority, to translate policy harms into electoral risks benefitting both regulated entities and the party.[25]

The specter of public oversight hearings deters against deviations in bureaucratic policymaking.[26] A major research question is whether public oversight is responsive to administrative procedures.[27] Congress is able to control policymaking determined through bureaucratic inquiries

[25] Eric Schickler & Andrew Rich, *Party Government in the House Reconsidered: A Response to Cox and McCubbins*, 41 Am. J. Pol. Sci. (1997) at 1387–1394; Gary Cox & Mathew D. McCubbins, *Toward a Theory of Legislative Rules Changes: Assessing Schickler and Rich's Evidence*, 41 Am. J. Pol. Sci. (1997) at 1376–1383.

[26] Brian Feinstein, *Avoiding Oversight: Legislator Preferences & Congressional Monitoring of the Administrative State*, 8 J. L. Econ. & Pol'y (2011). It is important to note that per McCubbins & Schwartz (1984), the effectiveness of congressional hearings is not an invalidation of their theory, for hearings may be *ex ante* informed through fire alarms. Further, McCubbins & Schwartz (1984) clarify that "formal" oversight refers to committees and subcommittees with specific oversight jurisdiction. David E. Lewis, *Revisiting the Administrative Presidency: Policy, Patronage, and Administrative Competence*, 39 Pres. Stud. Qrtrly (2009), at 60–73.

[27] *See* Arnaud Dellis & Mandar Oak, *Subpoena Power and Informational Lobbying*, J. Theor. Polit. (2020), at doi: 10.1177/0951629819892339, notes 3 & 4.

McCubbins & Schwartz, *supra* note 5 at 165; For recent applications of the fire-alarm model to oversight of federal law enforcement, *see* Daniel Richman, *Federal Criminal*

by incentivizing agency watchdogs, regulated parties, and their organized interests to set the public oversight agenda of Congress. As McNollGast write, "political leaders assign relative degrees of importance to the constituents whose interests are at stake in an administrative proceeding and thereby channel an agency's decisions toward the substantive outcomes that are most favored by those who are intended to be benefited by the policy."[28] Such agenda-setting curbs bureaucratic drift through oversight investigations and hearings which secure electoral rewards for key oversight committee members.[29]

To the extent police-patrol monitoring is a form of *ex post* sanction, such direct monitoring is not mutually exclusive from remote monitoring through administrative procedures in the sense illustrated by the concept of fire-alarm oversight.[30] I expect that administrative procedures are related to the fact-gathering and hearing activity of committees. If the expectation is viable, measuring oversight through hearings is a useful proxy for the efficacy of administrative procedures. In particular, interested parties with standing to raise procedural harms would be expected to remediate those harms by setting the issue agenda for committees with oversight jurisdiction. In this sense, when the Inspector General Act mandates Inspectors General report semi-annually to Congress or major policy reforms like the Resource Conservation and Recovery Act requires the Government Accountability Office to submit a report within a statutory time period, those requirements ensure that parties empowered to investigate and audit programs and policies are conditioned to share their investigative findings with committees with appropriate oversight jurisdiction.

We would also expect that interested parties, whether the private sector or officials like Inspectors General, would strategically provide information to oversight committees whose incentive is to invest resources only in

Law, Congressional Delegation, and Enforcement Discretion, 46 UCLA L. Rev. 757 (1999). Rachel E. Barkow, *Administering Crime*, 52 UCLA L. Rev. 715 (2005).

[28] McNollGast 1987, *supra* note 5 at 244; *accord* McCubbins & Schwartz, *supra* note 5 at 168 ("[u]nder a fire-alarm policy, by contrast, potential supporters can in most cases bring to congressmen's attention any violations that harm them and for which they have received no adequate remedy through the executive or judicial branch").

[29] McCubbins & Schwartz, *supra* note 5 at 167.

[30] Administrative procedures "increase the efficacy of ex post sanctions". McNollGast 1987, *supra* note 5 at 259.

matters that permit position-taking, credit-claiming, and issue advertising. Otherwise, we should expect that mere procedural harms can be resolved through bureaucratic or judicial review mechanisms. Oversight hearings, themselves proxies for committee investigative activity after effective interested party agenda-setting, are expected to maximize electoral benefits and minimize resource costs for oversight committee chairs and members. This expectation would distinguish the hearing activities of a full oversight committee (House Oversight and Reform) or an oversight subcommittee (House Energy and Commerce subcommittee on oversight and investigations) from the hearings held by committees or subcommittees without oversight jurisdiction established by rule, e.g., the Senate Appropriations Committee. As described below, I expect committees and subcommittees with oversight jurisdiction to maximize the number of hearings conducted while minimizing the amount of time each hearing lasts.

2.1 Motivations to Delegate: Maximal Electoral Rewards for Minimum Work

As stated above, I expect congressional committees (inclusive of subcommittees) with oversight jurisdiction to hold public hearings in a manner that maximizes electoral benefits and minimizes resource costs and tradeoffs from electoral benefits. This decision-making framework is accepted by both McNollGast and Aberbach. For instance, Aberbach argues, "[r]eelection-seeking political entrepreneurs spend their time and resources on activities yielding the most payoff[.]"[31] McNollGast write, "an important function of administrative procedures is to provide a means of inducing bureaucratic compliance that does not require the time, effort, and resources of political actors."[32] McCubbins and Schwartz similarly argue, "a fire-alarm policy enables congressmen to spend less time on oversight, leaving more time for other profitable activities, or to spend the same time on more personally profitable oversight activities—on addressing complaints by potential supporters."[33]

[31] Aberbach, *supra* note at 23 at 189.

[32] McNollGast 1987, *supra* note 5 at 254.

[33] McCubbins & Schwartz, *supra* note 5 at 168. The work of Keith Krehbiel focuses on these electoral motivations. *See* Keith Krehbiel, *Information and Legislative Organization* (1991); Keith Krehbiel, *Where's the Party?* 23 British J. Pol. Sci. at 235–266 (1993); Keith Krehbiel, *Institutional and Partisan Sources of Gridlock: A Theory of Divided and*

This decision-making framework concerning congressional motivations for oversight hearings mirrors the legislative developments which formalized oversight of the bureaucracy through congressional rules and administrative procedures. The Legislative Reorganization Act of 1946 transferred investigative and adjudicative functions of Congress by establishing the Federal Tort Claims Act and abolishing the Committee on Claims due to "[t]he magnitude of the task of considering and disposing of private claims,"[34] thus reserving those adjudicative determinations to the Court of Claims.

In the Senate report supporting the Legislative Reorganization Act of 1946, a section titled "Saving congressional time" stated, "Congress is overburdened by many local and private matters which divert its attention from national policy making and which it ought not to have to consider.... It serves as a tribunal for the settlement of private claims.... S. 2177 bans the introduction in either House of private claims and pension bills, bridge bills, and other local and private legislation. Title IV provides for the administrative and judicial adjustment of tort claims against the United States which Congress is poorly equipped to settle."[35] The Senate Government Operations report issued subsequent to the Legislative Reorganization Act of 1970 found that "[t]he more publicity given hearings the more effective means of oversight they usually are. Good publicity not only attracts greater attention by Members of Congress, but also puts additional pressure on agencies to reform their practices."[36]

Legislative reorganization simultaneously reduced resource costs to Congress when conducting oversight while maximizing public-facing activities associated with oversight. Congressional investigations and hearings, with their attendant staffing and preparation requirements, appear costly[37] when compared to other statutory tools that restrict use of funds,

Unified Government, 8 J. Theor. Pol. 1–40 (1996) (finding that cross-branch ideological conflict motivates oversight activity); Keith Krehbiel, *Pivotal Politics: A Theory of U.S. Lawmaking* (1998) (same).

34 Senate Report, *supra* note 35 at 30.

35 Senate Report 1400 on S. 2177 (1946) at 7.

36 *See* Senate Government Operations Report, *supra* note 54 in Chapter 2 at 52.

37 Robert McGrath, *Congressional Oversight Hearings and Policy Control*, 38 Leg. Stud. Qrtrly (2013) at 349–376.

such as appropriations riders,[38] or regulatory review provisions[39] that add procedural burdens to the federal decision-making process. Yet hearings are the most explicit mechanism for members of oversight committees to go public, credit claim and position take.[40] Scholars have argued that oversight committee and subcommittee hearings are the "most firmly rooted"[41] form of oversight.[42] A body of literature would suggest that evidence of Congress reducing its oversight workload is evidence congressional capacity to cabin the bureaucracy is diminishing.[43] Further, serving on a congressional oversight committee does not have clear electoral benefits for individual members.[44] This literature does not view congressional capacity for control of the bureaucracy as a model of the contingent nature of oversight hearings on administrative procedures.

[38] Jason MacDonald, *Limitation Riders and Congressional Influence over Bureaucratic Policy Decisions*, 104 Am. Pol. Sci. R. (2010) at 766.

[39] Susan Dudley, *Improving Regulatory Accountability: Lessons from the Past and Prospects for the Future*, 65 Case Western L. Rev. (2015) at 1027–1057.

[40] *See* Mayhew (1974), note 45, *supra*.

[41] Feinstein (2009), *supra* note 44.

[42] The Supreme Court has never upheld congressional oversight on grounds of separation of powers or political control—the justifications specified by political scientists and other scholars. The oversight power was understood as antecedent to the legislative power such that Congress could not exercise its Article I implied powers to pass all laws "necessary and proper" to the execution of Article I's enumerated powers without the ability to conduct inquiries, studies and examinations emblematized by investigations. But this legal justification is simply about the scope of legislative power and concerned Congress's power to investigate private individuals and companies, not government agencies. *See Oklahoma Press Publishing v. Walling* (1946) (citing *McGrain v. Daugherty* as a justification for an agency's use of investigations as a proper delegation of legislative power). It would be problematic for the Supreme Court to determine that Congress had a power to investigate the executive and simultaneously delegate that power to the executive (to presumably investigate itself, as opposed to investigating individuals and companies for law enforcement purposes, which it does with regularity). It is therefore an unanswered question whether Congress has any constitutional power to investigate executive branch agencies which are themselves quasi-legislative, quasi-judicial creatures of the legislature itself.

[43] Seymour Scher, *Conditions for Legislative Control*, 25 J. of Polit. 526–551 (1963); Morris Ogul, *Congress Oversees the Bureaucracy* (1976); Theodore Lowi, *The End of Liberalism* (1969); Lawrence Dodd & Richard Schott, *Congress and the Administrative State* (1979); David C.W. Parker & Matthew Dull, *Divided We Quarrel: The Politics of Congressional Investigations*, 34 Leg. Stud. Qtrly (2009) at 319–345.

[44] Brian Feinstein, *Dissertation: Oversight, Despite the Odds: Assessing Congressional Committee Hearings as a Means of Control over the Federal Bureaucracy* (2009).

Thus competing literatures might agree that the need for lawmakers to obtain information necessary to make policy decisions is considered secondary to the opportunity to trumpet the ideologies of important committee members and provide media attention to both constituent concerns as well as the committee members themselves.[45] And both literatures might agree that public oversight hearings permit issue advertising, position-taking, and credit-claiming.[46] But scholars disagree as to whether this evidence suggests diminished or heightened legislative capacity over the bureaucracy.

I propose to show that the evidence of members using public oversight activities in a manner that maximizes their electoral interests reflects heightened congressional capacity for oversight by viewing such public activities as causally related to the establishment of administrative procedures.

2.2 *Administrative Procedures Serve a Monitoring Function by Attaching Requirements to Delegation That Maximize Electoral Preferences*

Statutes delegate authority and establish rules. Rules both set forth the public policy goals of bureaucratic authority to regulate as well as regulate how that authority can be administered. Rules concerning administration of policymaking are administrative procedures. Administrative procedures have the force of law because they are contained in statutes signed by the president. When regulated parties file suits, go to the media, or have their trade associations lobby (pull fire alarms to alert congressional committees of procedural violations by the bureaucracy), subsequent direct congressional activity (which can serve as police patrols) can be fully motivated by electoral preferences yet nevertheless, by exposing agency conduct, serve to curb agency drift from the policy preferences of the congressional majority. By establishing administrative procedures, Congress can enhance

[45] David, *Mayhew Congress: The Electoral Connection* (1974) (hereinafter "Mayhew 1974"); David Mayhew, *Divided We Govern: Party Control, Lawmaking, and Investigations*, 1946–1990 (2005); Walter J. Jatkowski, *Dissertation. Political and Policy Issue Context & Contexts and Policy Information: Conditional Effects on Information in Congressional Hearings* (2012).

[46] Mayhew 1974, *supra* note 45.

its electoral interests in issue advertising, position-taking, and credit-claiming while also ensuring the bureaucracy makes preferred public policy.

The standard model of delegation and oversight is that because "not every decision can be made by [C]ongress," "the delegation of authority to the agencies" is necessary.[47] Delegation is attractive in the oversight context because while partisanship within Congress causes legislative inertia, it does not affect investigative and regulatory activity by agencies.[48] As McNollGast write, "political actors can be expected to engage in delegation even if they find perfect compliance to be excessively costly. Delegation confers a benefit by expanding the scope of politically relevant activity available to them."[49] If no such delegation occurs, then it challenges the picture of Congress preferring to monitor agents indirectly through procedure. This is so because Congress would be constrained to *directly* monitor political officials and the private sphere—policy targets considered distinct from the traditional bureaucracy—rather than instrumentalize its monitoring through bureaucratic procedures. Further, it would beg the question, raised by Epstein and O'Halloran, why Congress would rely on delegation and related procedures in one context of policymaking but not in another. But if such delegation can be shown, then monitoring the bureaucracy involves monitoring the bureaucratic implementation of public policy in at least three forms: conducting investigations of the private sphere, issuing legislative rules and orders with the force of law that bind the private sphere, and investigating political officials' compliance with statutory responsibilities ("ministerial duties"). Another way of solving the key research question is to determine whether political monitoring of the bureaucracy is inclusive of these three forms of policymaking.

[47] Senate Government Operations report, *supra* note 54 in Chapter 2 at 6. Under the nondelegation doctrine, Congress may delegate the legislative decision-making power established under Article I, §1 of the Constitution to agencies, but only if it "lay[s] down by legislative act an intelligible principle to which the person or body authorized to [act] is directed to conform." *Whitman v. American Trucking Assoc.*, 531 U.S. 457, 472 (2001) (quoting *J.W. Hampton Jr. & Co. v. United States*, 276 U.S. 394, 409 (1928)).

[48] *See* Dudley, *supra* note 39.

[49] McNollGast 1987, *supra* note 5 at 247.

Administrative Subpoenas Issued by the Bureaucracy over the Private Sector Would Be Expected to Reduce Oversight Workload

In a report to Congress, the U.S. Department of Justice defined an "administrative subpoena" to include all powers "Congress has granted to federal agencies to make an administrative or civil investigatory demand compelling document production or testimony."[50] Excluded from the definition of an administrative subpoena are "Grand jury subpoenas, administrative law judge subpoenas, and investigative authorities requiring judicial approval."[51] In the Department of Justice's own cognizance, administrative subpoenas are separate from politically supervised law enforcement tools. As stated above, the Supreme Court has recognized administrative subpoenas as "within the power of Congress to command."[52] The Supreme Court has distinguished administrative subpoenas from law enforcement subpoenas, holding administrative subpoenas, "are not to be construed as authorizing enforcement."[53] Further, in defending administrative subpoenas as legislative in nature, the Court held that "to deny the validity of the orders would be in effect to deny not only Congress' power to enact the provisions sustaining them, but also its authority to delegate effective power to investigate violations of its own laws, if not perhaps also its own power to make such investigations."[54]

My interest in administrative subpoenas, then, is due to the fact that they represent an almost pure form of congressional delegation not examined in the literature: Congress's delegation of investigations versus rulemaking. Administrative procedures in the form of statutes authorizing judicially enforceable information requests by the bureaucracy are an indicator[55] of Congress's delegation of investigative powers. If agency administrative subpoena power is delegated by Congress, we should

[50] U.S. Department of Justice, Report to Congress on the Use of Administrative Subpoena Authorities by executive branch Agencies and Entities, Pursuant to P.L. 106-55, Section 7, http://www.justice.gov/archive/olp/rpt_to_congress.htm.

[51] *Id.*

[52] *Oklahoma Press Pub. Co. v. Walling*, 327 U.S. 186, 201 (1946).

[53] *Id.*

[54] *Id.*

[55] John Gerring, *Mere Description*, 42 British J. of Polit. Sci. (2012) at 726.

observe a causal relationship between congressional delegation of investigative powers and the reduction of Congress's resources committed to investigative activities. Further, bureaucratic investigations should inform congressional oversight activity. If agency investigations were part of law enforcement rather than truly legislative, we should expect Congress's passage of administrative subpoena-authorizing statutes to have no effect on reducing Congress's subsequent electoral efficiency preference.[56]

I expect this for two reasons. First, oversight committees are aware of ethical[57] and legal restrictions treating law enforcement investigations differently than policymaking activities.[58] Congressional committees have intervened in administrative subpoenas[59] while generally not doing so concerning criminal investigations.[60] Second, constitutional procedures,

[56] Terry M. Moe, *Congressional Controls of the Bureaucracy: An Assessment of the Positive Theory of 'Congressional Dominance*, 12 Leg. Stud. Qrtrly (1987) at 477–479 ("because legislators are centrally concerned with reelection, they are quite unconcerned with bureaucratic behavior except as it affects the net benefits flowing to their districts").

[57] Ethics Manual for Members, Officers, and Employees of the U.S. House of Representatives, Committee on Standards of Official Conduct, 102nd Cong., 2d Sess. 241 (1993); U.S. Senate Rule 43 (1992).

[58] *Compare SEC v. Wheeling-Pittsburgh Steel Corp*, 482 F. Supp 555 (W.D. Pa. 1979), vacated and remanded, 648 F.2d 118 (3d Cir. 1981) (*en banc*) ("we cannot simply avert our eyes from the realities of the political world: members of Congress are requested to, and do in fact, intrude, in varying degrees, in administrative proceedings") to Letter to Hon. John D. Dingell Chairman, House Subcommittee on Oversight and Investigation, Committee on Energy and Commerce, from Attorney General William French Smith, dated Nov. 30, 1982, reprinted in H. Rept. No. 97-968 at 37–38 (opining that congressional intervention in law enforcement investigations "would prejudice the cause of effective law enforcement").

[59] *See e.g.*, Comment, *Judicial Restriction on Improper Congressional Influence in Administrative Influence in Administrative Decision-making: A Defense of the Pillsbury Doctrine*, 6 J. Law & Polit. 135, 154 (1989) (cited in Congressional Research Service, CRS Report for Congress No. RL32113, *Congressional Intervention in the Administrative Process: Legal and Ethics Considerations* (2003) at 32); *Sinclair v. United States*, 279 U.S. 263, 294 (1929).

[60] Todd David Peterson, *Congressional Oversight of Open Criminal Investigations*, 77 Notre Dame L. Rev. 1373, 1410 (2002) ("Congress seems generally to have been respectful of the need to protect material contained in open criminal investigative files. There is almost no precedent for Congress attempting to subpoena such material, and even fewer examples of the DOJ actually producing such documents").

rather than administrative procedures, attach to law enforcement investigations.[61] Therefore, with law enforcement investigations, Congress would be limited to information obtained by statutory reporting requirements to designated committees and would be unable to rely upon administrative procedures for information concerning policy infractions.[62]

When this framework is applied to congressional oversight hearings, I would expect there to be a diminishing marginal utility of a hearing's publicity value after a certain amount of time which informs my first hypothesis:

Hypothesis 1: Delegation of investigative powers in the form of statutes authorizing administrative subpoenas should permit Congress to conduct more oversight hearings at reduced duration per hearing.

The Paired Strategies of the Administrative Procedure Act and the Legislative Reorganization Act: Committee Oversight Structure to Reward Agenda-Setting

Political scientists have not interpreted the Administrative Procedure Act as connected to its legislative twin, the Legislative Reorganization Act of 1946. One implication of this bifurcation is a simplified causal story that says Congress delegates policymaking to the bureaucracy and prefers to monitor that policymaking through administrative procedures, which, in practical terms, means a company sues an agency under the Administrative Procedure Act when the agency drifts from the policy bargain struck between Congress, the president, and the relevant special interest constituents. The difficulty with this story is it does not explain how Congress obtains information subsequently relied upon for its oversight hearings. It assumes that congressional oversight committees are designed to build investigative dockets from which to aggressively gather facts, probe leads, and hold hearings with the aim of writing enlightened laws.

McNollGast state "[c]onstituency service has become an increasingly important activity of members of Congress in the postwar era, to the point where it now accounts for more than half of the staff effort in

61 *Oklahoma Press supra* note 46 in Chapter 2 at 195 (administrative procedures "present no question of actual search and seizure"), or, *id.* at 208 (risk of "self-incrimination").

62 *Ins v. Chadha*, 462 U.S. 919, 955 n.19 (1983).

Congress[.]"[63] But if fire-alarm-pulling constituents do not know which committees have jurisdiction over a given procedural harm, congressional capacity for oversight cannot be robust under a fire-alarm system. Scholars have found that overlap in the oversight jurisdiction of multiple committees provides electoral rewards to individual members but undermines Congress's ability to mediate presidential control of the bureaucracy.[64] Jurisdictional overlap causes "the splintering of power over a larger number of distinct actors and different agencies, and more episodes of overlapping jurisdiction among them."[65]

Crucial to the procedural link developed through political analysis of the APA is the jurisdictional link created by the 1946 LRA. While the APA provides fire-alarm rights that can be asserted occasionally, the LRA, by creating permanent committees with oversight jurisdiction established by rules, empowers the more consistent fire-alarm pullers like Inspectors General or the Comptroller General to ensure that the environment of agency decision-making mirrors the political conditions in which Congress issued the legislation. Senator LaFollette, the lead architect of the Legislative Reorganization Act of 1946 stated, "[p]ublic affairs are now handled by a host of administrative agencies headed by nonelected officials, with only casual oversight by Congress."[66] LaFollette, as if responding to those scholars who overlook the LRA, sought to "simplify the committee structure" and "to correlate it with the departments and agencies of the Federal Government."[67] As McCubbins & Schwartz suggest, there is an argument that modern congressional oversight is an *ex post* reaction to administrative governance rather than an *ex ante* mechanism for guiding statutory enforcement.[68] If jurisdictional

[63] McNollGast 1987, *supra* note 5, at 250.

[64] Joshua D. Clinton, David E. Lewis, & Jessica L. Selin, *Influencing the Bureaucracy: The Irony of Congressional Oversight*, 58 Am. J. Pol. Sci. (2014) at 387–401.

[65] Sean Farhang & Miranda Yaver, *Divided Government and the Fragmentation of American Law*, 60 Am. J. Pol. Sci. (2016) at 403, note 1.

[66] Senator LaFollette, Congressional Record (June 5, 1946), 6344.

[67] 1946 LRA, *supra* note 67 in Chapter 2.

[68] McCubbins & Schwartz, *supra* note 5 at 169 ("Congress [] respond[s] to the complexity of issues by … creating a large, expert congressional staff—one sufficiently large and expert, not only to help decide complex issues, but to help oversee a large, expert bureaucracy"). Because an executive branch agency is "a creature of statute" it "has no constitutional or common law existence or authority, but only those authorities

rules are a form of procedure under the LRA that mirrors administrative procedure under the APA, then motivations to delegate due to "new policy areas, salient public issues, and areas in which the consequences of ill-formed policy are politically disastrous … [which] provoke Congress to delegate more power to executive agents"[69] also present incentives for Congress to ensure that it provides fire-alarm rights to those who act as beneficiaries of legislative power and fiduciaries of the enacting coalition's interpretation of that power.

Unlike regulated constituents, Inspectors General confirmed by the Senate have no terms, effectively giving them lifetime appointments, and the Comptroller General serves a 15-year term, guaranteeing that both Inspectors General and the Comptroller General have incentives to appease Congress throughout the political change in administrations. I expect these officers, more so than the occasional harmed constituent, to ensure the maintenance of the intent of the enacting coalition. The notion of the "intent" of the enacting coalition can be understood in more practical terms: who has jurisdiction over a given policy or program at a given agency? Inspectors General—who outlast presidents and committee chairs—are experts in setting the congressional oversight agenda because the source of their power rests on their ability to dictate which committee or subcommittee has appropriate jurisdictional authority. I therefore seek to test in Chapter 4 the following additional hypothesis consistent with the decision-making framework identified above:

Hypothesis 2: Delegation of investigative powers to Inspectors General should permit Congress to conduct more oversight hearings at reduced duration per hearing.

conferred upon it by Congress." *Michigan v. EPA*, 268 F.3d 1075, 1081 (D.C. Cir. 2001).

[69] Epstein & O'Halloran 1999a, *supra* note 8 at 710.

CHAPTER 4

The Politics of Overseeing the Administrative State

The politics of delegation and oversight signify the Janus-faced countenance of American administrative law. Congressional oversight is an American political phenomenon whose significance arises as a result of Congress's delegation of policymaking authority to the bureaucracy.[1] The concept of oversight describes the process of congressional supervision and control of legislative power as exercised by congressional agents located beyond the halls of Congress.[2] In the abstract, Congress can only legitimately exercise political control over the bureaucracy if the

[1] Robert McGrath, *Congressional Oversight Hearings and Policy Control*, 38 Leg. Stud. Qrtl'y at 349, 350 (2013) ("oversight is made necessary by the ubiquity of delegation in a modern system of government"). Legal scholars and political scientists often mean different things when discussing "delegation" by Congress. For legal scholars, delegation means vesting legislative power in another branch of government, notably the executive branch and thus has constitutional implications. *See* Julian D. Mortenson & Nicholas Bagley, *Delegation at the Founding*, 121 Colum. L. Rev. 277, 332–349 (2021) (hereinafter "Mortenson & Bagley"). For political scientists, delegation means Congress's assignment to another branch the responsibility to further develop public policy. Roderick Kiewiet & Mathew McCubbins, *The Logic of Delegation* (1991). Some political scientists understand delegation in terms of power while viewing the bureaucracy as itself a legislative institution. *See* David Epstein & Sharyn O'Halloran, *Delegating Powers: A Transaction Cost Politics Approach to Policy Making Under Separate Powers* (1999). Mathew McCubbins, Roger Noll, & Barry Weingast, *Administrative Procedures as Instruments of Political Control*, 3 J. L. Econ. & Org. 243 (1987).

[2] McGrath, *supra* note 1.

D. Z. Epstein, *The Investigative State: Regulatory Oversight in the United States*, https://doi.org/10.1007/978-3-031-38461-5_4

bureaucracy is acting under legislative auspices.[3] The intrinsic relationship between oversight and delegation further stands on the fact that oversight informs regulatory policy extralegally—that is, it relies on legislative actions other than laws subject to bicameralism and presentment. In this sense, oversight ensures delegated power remains subject to legislative control notwithstanding the agents or agencies exercising such power being located within another branch of government.

Scholarly contributions to the empirical study of the politics of congressional oversight often rely on congressional hearings as a key indicator for making inferences and predictions about oversight.[4] And yet scholarly explanations for how hearings affect oversight can diverge within the American politics literature itself. Some scholars describe congressional oversight hearings in terms of the information they provide to members in crafting public policy.[5] Others, however, frame oversight hearings as less about information transmission to members than their serving a publicity function that reduces bureaucratic "infractions."[6] The literature distinguishes these institutional incentives for oversight ("ex post controls"[7] of "policy implementation by the agencies and officials of the executive branch"[8]) from behavioral member-level incentives ("ex ante strategies"[9] aimed toward "reelection-centered goals"[10]).

This chapter contributes to the empirical literature examining oversight in terms of congressional hearings but seeks to integrate the theoretical work on the role of administrative procedures into the strategy for

[3] Joshua Clinton, David E. Lewis, & Jennifer L. Selin, *Influencing the Bureaucracy: The Irony of Congressional Oversight*, 58 Am. J. Pol. Sci. (2014), 387–401.

[4] Daniel Diermeier & Timothy Feddersen, *Information and Congressional Hearings*, 44 Am. J. Pol. Sci. 51 (2000). Robert H. Davidson & Walter J. Oleszek, *Congress and Its Members* 357 (2006).

[5] Frank R. Baumgartner & Bryan D. Jones, *Agency Dynamics and Policy Subsystems*, 53 J. of Pol. 1044–1074 (1991); Frank R. Baumgartner & Bryan D. Jones, *Agendas and Instability in American Politics* (1993).

[6] Brian Feinstein, *Oversight, Despite the Odds: Assessing Congressional Committee Hearings as a Means of Control over the Federal Bureaucracy* (dissertation) (2009).

[7] McGrath, *supra* note 1.

[8] Dodd & Schott, *Congress and the Administrative State* (1979) at 156.

[9] *See e.g.*, McGrath, note 1 at 350.

[10] *Id.* at 352.

modeling the relationship between delegation and oversight. It nevertheless departs from the literature explaining oversight hearings as a source of policy by instead examining oversight hearings, both in terms of the number of hearings and individual hearing length as influenced by the electoral preferences of committee members.[11]

Oversight is informed by a tradeoff between Congress's institutional goal of controlling bureaucratic policy and the electoral interests of members. When faced with such tradeoffs, Congress can optimize both institutional goals and the electoral incentives of members through delegation. For instance, during the New Deal, when facing tension between public expectations of federal regulatory authority and Congress's own institutional resources, Congress delegated rulemaking authority to the bureaucracy. The conflict between the need for oversight and the electoral interests of members arose as a result of the prior decision to delegate legislative power in order to optimize both individual member and institutional interests. I, therefore, expect that Congress would choose the form of oversight that best resolves inefficiency resulting from the tradeoff between institutional expectations and member-level interests by delegating institutional resources (capacity) to maximize individual member's electoral incentives.

Over the last 75 years, Congress's revealed preference for oversight has changed from one where hearings typically lasted for over a day to one where Congress conducts more hearings by reducing the cost, in terms of duration, per hearing to significantly less than a day. If Congress can delegate institutional capacity, it can reduce costs associated with such capacity to maximize the electoral preferences of members. I therefore expect that variation in member-level electoral preferences will affect variation in the efficiency of Congress-level oversight hearings through the choice of legislative procedure. I predict that change in institutional-level, *ex post* oversight efficiency results from Congress's procedural choice to delegate its institutional capacity for oversight. If my theory is true, then variation in Congress's institutional structure, versus divided government, cameral differences between the House and the Senate, polarization, or

[11] Kenneth Lowande & Justin Peck, *Congressional Investigations and the Electoral Connection*, 33 J. L. Econ. & Org. (2017); Austin Bussing & Michael Pomirchy, *Congressional Oversight and Electoral Accountability* (Aug. 9, 2021) at 1 (finding electoral considerations to be a key driver of variation in oversight activity).

ideological distance between committee medians and the bureaucracy,[12] is the key causal predictor of efficiency in congressional oversight hearings.[13] Those factors may be relevant to the timing or content of a given hearing but they do not explain the institutional-level phenomenon where the length of time per oversight hearing decreases as the number of total oversight hearings increases.

1 Punctuated Delegation: The Political Development of the Administrative State

My novel approach to modeling oversight reveals the key research question I seek to address: why, as Fig. 2, shows, do oversight hearings appear to change in the 95th Congress (and 1978 specifically)? In earlier chapters, I find that the suspected change in 1978 was preceded by decades of changes in the subject matter of investigative committees. Prior to 1978, congressional committees with investigative authority focused their investigations and hearings on the need to regulate interstate commercial activities, with the notion of "oversight" hearings focused on the executive branch appearing around the 1940s.

These historical insights are relevant to framing my empirical examination of the relationship between delegation and oversight. The political and legal development of the modern bureaucracy, from the Interstate Commerce Commission (1887) to the Federal Trade Commission (1914), the Securities and Exchange Commission and Federal Communications Commission (1934), and the National Labor Relations Board (1935), evidences a pattern of punctuated delegation: first, Congress delegated to congressional committees the authority to investigate, over several legislative sessions, public welfare problems arising from national commercial activity; second, based on investigative findings made from these committee probes, Congress creates an agency, not so unlike a select committee, tasked with investigative and adjudicative powers while

[12] E.g., Rachel Augustine Potter & Kevin Lowande, *Congressional Oversight Revisited: Policy and Procedure in Agency Rulemaking*, J. of Politics (2020).

[13] Lowande and Peck, *supra* note 11, show, for instance, that passage of the 17th Amendment (a legal change to Congress), not divided government, predicted changes in Senate oversight activities, viz., as an opportunity to advance electoral interests.

reserving rulemaking to Congress[14]; third, Congress eventually delegates rulemaking to the agency; and fourth, the relevant congressional investigative committees shift from investigating businesses or writing policy to conducting oversight over the agency's policymaking.

It is from this history that I suspect the change in congressional oversight that occurred in the aftermath of Watergate is an extension of the pattern of delegation that began in the nineteenth century: Congress, after delegating its investigative and rulemaking powers to the bureaucracy eventually delegates oversight responsibilities to the bureaucracy itself.[15] The 95th Congress statutorily formalized Inspectors General with the power to police the bureaucracy, created the Civil Service Commission, and enacted the Ethics in Government Act—all of which subjected executive branch officials and their programs to scrutiny and incentivized bureaucratic officers to inform Congress about waste, fraud, abuse or malfeasance.

In this chapter, I test my theory that over this near-century period, Congress has increasingly delegated the hard work of monitoring the bureaucracy to the bureaucracy itself (through laws like the Inspector General Act) and to private parties (through statutes like the Administrative Procedure Act).[16] That prediction is entirely consistent with the theory that Congress prefers to monitor the bureaucracy by responding

[14] *Marshall Field & Co. v. Clark*, 143 U.S. 649, 693–694 (1892) ("[t]he true distinction... is between the delegation of power to make the law, which necessarily involves a discretion as to what it shall be, and conferring authority or discretion as to its execution, to be exercised under and in pursuance of the law. The first cannot be done; to the latter no valid objection can be made") (internal quotations omitted); *Interstate Commerce Commission v. Cincinnati, N. O. & T. P. R. Co.*, 167 U.S. 479, 501 (1897) ("the power given is the power to execute and enforce, not to legislate. The power given is partly judicial, partly executive and administrative, but not legislative"); *Humphrey's Ex'r v. United States*, 295 U.S. 602, 624 (1935) ("It is charged with the enforcement of no policy except the policy of the law. Its duties are neither political nor executive, but predominantly quasi-judicial and quasi-legislative. Like the Interstate Commerce Commission, its members are called upon to exercise the trained judgment of a body of experts 'appointed by law and informed by experience.'") (internal citation omitted).

[15] Data on House and Senate investigations from 1789 to 1948 reflect that only 500 congressional investigations of the executive branch occurred during this period largely due to the "meager" "scope and scale of administrative activity on the part of the federal government" during this time. Lowande and Peck, *supra* note 11 at 7.

[16] *See* note 14 *supra*.

to fire alarms.[17] The difference, or rather an addition, of my theory to the fire-alarm theory is two-fold: first, I hypothesize that the predictive errors associated with the congressional choice to delegate legislative power, once conditioned by the institutional need to monitor delegation, will predict a subsequent congressional choice to delegate the monitoring, or "oversight", of delegation; and second, I suspect that the electoral interests of members underlie Congress's institutional choice to delegate oversight, which reduces institutional costs of monitoring the bureaucracy and allows faster, more numerous, congressional oversight hearings per year. Not only do "members value oversight hearings primarily as opportunities to make well-publicized political statements aimed at important constituent groups"[18] but that member preference is maximized through delegation of oversight capacity to the bureaucracy which allows oversight hearings to more efficiently promote electoral interests.

2 Ideological Motivations for Oversight, Electoral Explanations for Its Delegation

If oversight advances electoral interests, why would Congress prefer to lower the costs associated with monitoring? It is well-established in the literature that Congress delegates the legislative power of rule-making because of capacity constraints and conducts oversight over such delegation to move public policy toward its preferred ideology.[19] This institutional theory predicts that if Congress is freed up to obtain public policy information through its agents in the bureaucracy and the regulated community, then congressional oversight hearings can be more efficiently utilized to serve Congress's ideological interests.[20] While institutional motivations for oversight can be explained ideologically, for instance, in terms of the need for checks and balances, to counter the

[17] Mathew D. McCubbins & Thomas Schwartz, *Congressional Oversight Overlooked: Police Patrols Versus Fire Alarms*, 28 Am. J. Pol. Sci. at 165–179 (1984).

[18] Bussing and Pomirchy, *supra* note 11 at 5 (citing Ju Yeon Park, *When Do Politicians Grandstand? Measuring Message Politics in Committee Hearings*, 83 J. of Politics (2021)).

[19] Alexander Bolton & Sharece Thrower, *Legislative Capacity and Executive Unilateralism*, 60 Am. J. Pol. Sci. 649, 652 (2016).

[20] *Id.* Note here that by delegating oversight, the distinction in the literature between *ex ante* versus *ex post* oversight becomes less relevant as *ex ante* procedures secure *ex post* agenda-setting by delegates.

expansion of presidential power, or to ensure bureaucratic policy accords with the policy preferences of the majority party in Congress, such descriptions would not explain the decision to further delegate (at least some of) Congress's oversight capacity itself. Consistent with the work of others, I assume that while ideology predicts oversight over bureaucratic policy, the decision to delegate oversight (capacity for ideological control over policy) in order to achieve more, yet quicker, oversight hearings is dependent upon the expectation that oversight hearings for issue identification, credit-claiming, and position-taking advances members' reelection interests.[21] The implication of this theory is that congressional oversight hearings *are* an "exercise in congressional position taking, one that serves members' electoral interests" *and* influence interbranch relationships and the president's political capital.[22] As Kriner and Schickler explain, "the individual members who are most active in spearheading an investigation are likely to gain publicity that is often an individual benefit—helping boost their reelection and personal power—even as they contribute to the collective good of congressional power."[23]

3 Political Control over Delegation Through the Electoral Connection

My strategy for modeling the effects of delegation on oversight departs from traditional approaches that examine delegation via rulemaking[24] by instead focusing on the delegation of the legislative power to investigate—the historically first legislative power to be delegated. The mid-twentieth-century Supreme Court considered both agency investigations aimed to determine whether a private party's conduct was subject to a

[21] Gray W. Cox & Mathew D. *McCubbins, Legislative Leviathan: Party Government in the U.S. House of Representatives* (1993).

[22] Douglas L. Kriner & Eric Schickler, *Investigating the President: Committee Probes and Presidential Approval, 1953–2006*, 76 J. of Pol. (2014) at 521.

[23] *Id.* at 522.

[24] *See e.g.*, Brian Libgober, *Meetings, Comments, and the Distributive Politics of Rulemaking*, 15 Qrtly J. of Pol. Sci. 449, 450 (2020) (conflating "regulation" with "rulemaking"); *accord. id.* at 451 ("[i]n order to finalize a regulation, agencies must publish an official proposal and consider feedback in the form of written letters"). But agencies regulate through requests for information, subpoenas, sanctions, fines, and orders without public notice and comment.

particular statute and whether that party violated the statute as part of the "legislative power."[25] This is arguably distinct from law enforcement activity carried out under the supervision of the president, viz., "to prove a pending charge or complaint" and seek legal consequences for that party's failure to meet its obligations.[26]

Administrative subpoenas provide a fertile area for examining delegation as well as measuring the utility of administrative procedures as instruments of political control. Subsequent to the Supreme Court's *Oklahoma Press Publishing* decision, Congress enacted the Administrative Procedure Act (APA), which McNollgast highlights as exemplar of their theory that administrative procedures are Congress's preferred tool for controlling the bureaucracy.[27] As applied to agency subpoenas as legislative delegations, the APA requires advanced public statements by the agency addressing both the question of whether a statute applies to certain conduct as well as the standards governing a determination that the law was violated. And yet the Supreme Court has never determined that the APA's rulemaking requirements apply in advance of administrative subpoenas nor have regulated parties argued that rulemaking applies to agency determinations that a law governs some conduct, even when such a principle strikes at the core of the power to prescribe the duties by which citizens are regulated.[28]

In this chapter, I test whether congressional enactment of laws authorizing the bureaucracy to issue administrative subpoenas affects congressional oversight hearings. By also examining the effects of the enactment

[25] *Okla. Press Pub. Co. v. Walling*, 327 U.S. 186, 201–204 (1946).

[26] *Id.*, *supra* note 25 at 204–217.

[27] *See* McNollGast, *supra* notes 72 in Chapter 2, and note 5 in Chapter 3.

[28] *See Gundy v. United States*, 139 S. Ct. 2116, 2133 (2019) (Gorsuch, J., *dissenting*) ("[w]hen it came to the legislative power, the framers understood it to mean the power to adopt generally applicable rules of conduct governing future actions by private persons—the power to 'prescrib[e] the rules by which the duties and rights of every citizen are to be regulated,' or the power to "prescribe general rules for the government of society'"). In fact, regulated parties routinely do not rely on the original public disclosure requirements of the APA, 5 U.S.C. § 552(a)(1)(D), to argue that administrative subpoenas must be cabined by public justifications concerning their coverage and scope. Although outside the scope of this chapter, my work on pluralism in administrative law shows that administrative procedures only have legal effect when interested parties successfully argue as much before a court. *See e.g.*, Daniel Epstein, *Administrative Law Consequentialism*, CSAS Working Paper 21-10, *available at* https://administrativestate.gmu.edu/wp-content/uploads/sites/29/2021/02/Epstein-Administrative-Law-Consequentialism.pdf.

of the 1978 Inspector General Act, I can distinguish the effects of delegations of judicially unenforceable investigative powers over agency officials and programs (akin to oversight) from delegations of investigative powers over the private sphere enforceable in federal court (i.e., administrative subpoena powers). Inspectors General have both enforceable and unenforceable investigative powers. The Inspector General Act authorizes Inspectors General with administrative subpoena powers to investigate federal funding recipients for fraud while clearly stating that "procedures other than subpoenas shall be used by the Inspector General to obtain documents and information from Federal agencies."[29]

If congressional delegation of its investigative powers over the private sector, or over the bureaucracy in the form of the creation of Offices of Inspectors General, increases the electioneering opportunities for members through changes to the structure of oversight, then Congress retains control over its delegated powers. Under Epstein and O'Halloran's transaction-cost theory, delegated power is power for which Congress retains control over its exercise.[30] One visible distinction

[29] 5 U.S.C. Appx. § 6(a)(4). Inspectors General thus have incentives to appease Congress's oversight appetite in order to avoid any limitation to their law enforcement powers. *But see* Federal Housing Finance Agency Office of Inspector General, *Report of Administrative Inquiry into Allegations of Misconduct by the FHFA Director* (Nov. 29, 2018), *available at* https://www.fhfaoig.gov/sites/default/files/OIG-2019-001.pdf#page=4 (conceding the OIG's illegal use of an administrative subpoena against an employee). Note that here, the U.S. Attorney for the Eastern District of Virginia filed a petition to enforce the subpoena and the U.S. District Court enforced the subpoena.

[30] Epstein & O'Halloran (1999), *supra* note 1. The theory, as applied to delegation, views legislation as an incomplete contract due to the cost Congress, as principal, must absorb in seeking to prevent ambiguities or missing statutory provisions. Under systems of authority based on incomplete contracts, the contract itself is insufficient to judge institutional outcomes. *See* Grossman & Hart, *The Costs and Benefits of Ownership: A Theory of Vertical and Lateral Integration*, 94 J. Pol. Econ. 691–719 (1986). Instead, parties invest—outside the terms of the contract—as part of contractual bargaining. Because the transactions-cost approach requires that each party make non-contractual investments prior to contractual enactment, delegation must be made to an already-existing institution, whether the president or an administrative agency or department. Congress empowers the executive branch with discretion and both Congress and the executive branch entity fear an investment hold-up where Congress can threaten to cabin discretion and where the agency can threaten to shift allegiance to a presidential principal rather than a congressional one. Given that agency rulemaking is supervised by the president, which threatens the prerogatives of both parties, Congress delegates investigative power to the agency insulated from presidential control. The bargain is that the agency will enforce in ways

between Inspector General investigations of the bureaucracy and bureaucratic investigations of business is the lack of compulsory (judicially reviewable) procedures governing investigations of the bureaucracy. The fact that such delegation is not cabined by compulsory procedures is consistent with more historical forms of delegation by Congress, with the starkest example being the delegation of cameral powers to a committee. Attaching compulsory procedures to some authorization by Congress may reflect evidence that Congress has ceded control not just to an executive officer but to the executive agency that officer oversees and that, therefore, activities conducted under such authorization are properly supervised by the president, not Congress. Such findings would provide a basis for presuming that pre-enforcement subpoenas issued by administrative agencies are essential to the president's "duties as the head of the executive branch" and "to ensure that [the president's] subordinates serve the people effectively and in accordance with the policies that the people presumably elected the president to promote."[31]

Evidence that Congress grants its investigative powers over the private sector to the bureaucracy in the form of administrative subpoena authorizations without a residual benefit to its members' electoral preferences would suggest that Congress has ceded control over what would otherwise be considered the delegation of legislative power. Delegation of investigative powers is subject to the administrative procedure of judicial review and yet the use of administrative subpoenas by the executive branch may not increase congressional control. Concomitant with executive branch discretion is the limitation of congressional control over such discretion.[32] Evidence of structural changes in oversight may signal that members readily effectuate their electoral preferences without a prior legislative choice of administrative procedures—ones that typically limit executive branch discretion—by instead authorizing the bureaucracy with

consistent with Congress's ideological preferences while Congress protects the agency's independence from the president.

[31] *Collins v. Yellen*, 141 S. Ct. 1761, 1784 (2021). The present Supreme Court, in stark contrast to its *Oklahoma Press* predecessor, readily considers the authority "to issue subpoenas" as the exercise of "executive power". *Collins*, 141 S. Ct. at 1786.

[32] *Seila Law LLC v. Consumer Fin. Prot. Bureau*, 140 S. Ct. 2183, 2197 (2020); *Nixon v. Adm'r of Gen. Servs.*, 433 U.S. 425, 550–551 (1977) (Rehnquist, J., dissenting) ("[T]he President is made the sole repository of the executive powers of the United States[.]").

law enforcement powers committed to executive branch discretion.[33] If effects on the structure of oversight are not observed, the implications is that it is possible for Congress to maximize electoral incentives for members while ceding its power to the executive branch.[34]

Given this range of implications, the models explored in this chapter help contribute to the debate between theories of congressional dominance versus abdication. If Congress can pursue faster, more numerous oversight hearings by authorizing greater law enforcement power to the executive, then Congress has maximized its opportunities to publicize political infractions by the administration even as it has ceded actual control over legislative authority. In such a context, the executive may be actively policing statutory violations by regulated parties and the bureaucracy itself while nevertheless transmitting reports to Congress that help both members "garner media attention and portray the opposition party as corrupt or incompetent"[35] and Congress ensure public policy is consistent with its ideological preferences[36] even as the relevant executive branch decision-making is fully excluded from congressional purview.

4 Congressional Oversight in Decline or Optimally Efficient?

For most of the last century, House and Senate committees with oversight jurisdiction have followed a trend of holding more hearings while spending less time per hearing. This trend reflects members' preference for a form of oversight where holding more hearings is valued over the depth of individual hearings (Figs. 1 and 2).

The number of congressional oversight hearings, as measured by oversight committees and subcommittees, have generally increased over time. Hearings cost significant staff preparation time and keep members out of more electorally fruitful pursuits. But the norm for the committee staff and for chairs is to define their capacity for holding a presidential administration accountable by the number of hearings their committee

[33] McCubbins & Schwartz, *supra* note 17.

[34] *Accord*. Farhang, *supra* note 65 in Chapter 3 at 1541.

[35] Lowande & Peck, *supra* note 11 at 4.

[36] Kriner & Schickler (2014), *supra note* 22.

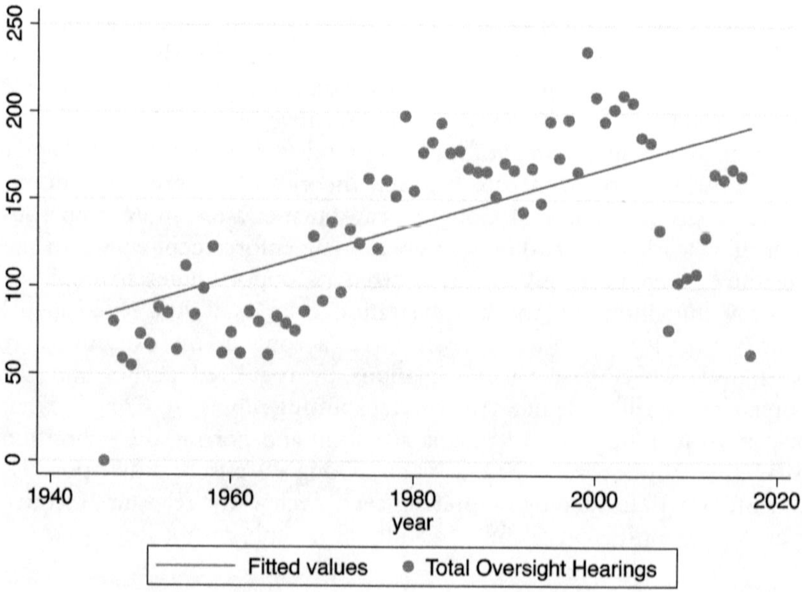

Fig. 1 Number of oversight hearings per year (1946–2020)

holds.[37] Because oversight hearings are a crucial way in which members earn media attention and because more junior members are often enticed with leadership roles on subcommittees, committee staff are intentional about witness selection and member attendance to ensure a committee or subcommittee chair can maximize credit-claiming and position-taking without trading off with the need to spend time on electorally beneficial activities.[38]

When evaluating the effectiveness of congressional oversight, scholars measure oversight in terms of legislative capacity.[39] Capacity is defined as "the ability of Congress to write legislation that could seriously constrain

[37] *See, e.g.*, The Lugar Center, *Congressional Oversight Hearing Index*, https://oversight-index.thelugarcenter.org/ (evaluating "devotion to oversight" based on the "pace" of oversight hearings).

[38] Walter J. Jatkowski, *Dissertation: Subsystem Contexts and Policy Information: Conditional Effects on Information in Congressional Hearings* (2012).

[39] Alexander Bolton & Sharece Thrower, *Checks in the Balance: Legislative Capacity and the Dynamics of Executive Power* (2021).

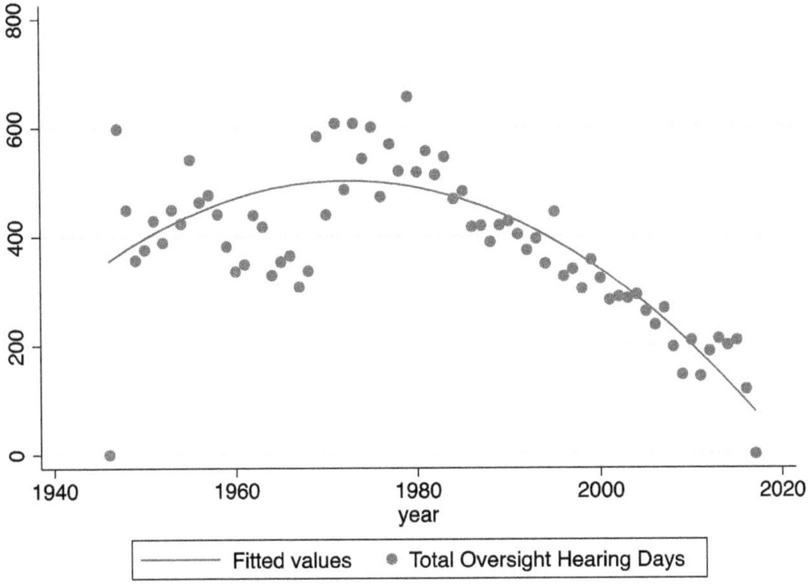

Fig. 2 Average hearing duration per year (1946–present)

the executive."[40] Given increasing oversight efficiency, we would expect that if Congress also prefers to conduct oversight by establishing administrative procedures, then those procedures should enhance efficiency by minimizing hearing duration (therefore permitting more hearings by a committee with oversight jurisdiction). While scholars like McNollgast do not specifically identify administrative procedures as controlling a delegatory grant of power by Congress, their understanding of procedure mirrors the Supreme Court's language of "an intelligible principle" necessary to constrain the bureaucracy when acting with legislative power.[41] Under this legal doctrine, so long as Congress authorizes the bureaucracy to act within constraints, no improper delegation of legislative power to the executive branch occurs.

[40] *Id. See also* Bolton and Thrower, *supra* note 19 at 653.

[41] *J.W. Hampton Jr. & Co. v. United States*, 276 U.S. 394, 409 (1928).

4.1 Bureaucratic Investigations as Legislative

Congress conducts oversight (monitoring the bureaucracy) but also investigates presidential administrations and the private sector. While contemporary oversight disputes present the legislative oversight power as justified whenever a congressional claim over the executive branch has a legislative purpose,[42] that understanding has evolved over history. The first century and a half of congressional investigations reflected that only congressional probes into the private sphere were considered relevant to a legislative purpose, as congressional inquiries into presidential administrations were always politically motivated.[43] Congress's private sector probes waned as administrative agencies were created initially with investigative and adjudicative powers subject to congressional approval and only later were empowered to write legislative rules.[44] Modern oversight thus arose from the political need to monitor the legislative activities of the bureaucracy yet was justified under the legal guise of the private sector inquiries Congress undertook in order to create regulatory agencies in the first place. Today, Congress's power to investigate the administration, the private sector and the bureaucracy itself has been assigned to Inspectors General, regulators, and litigants.[45] My particular interest is in the investigative powers known as administrative subpoenas, which the early twentieth-century Supreme Court has identified as "legislative in character."[46]

I distinguish Congress's power to investigate the president and his copartisans as well as its power to investigate corporations from its oversight power. Congress's ability to directly investigate an entity is derived from its impeachment power (investigating the president and the administration) or its necessary and proper clause power (investigating the private sphere).[47] Only when these investigative powers are delegated to the

[42] *Trump v. Mazars USA, LLP*, 140 S. Ct. 2019, 2031 (2020).

[43] Daniel Epstein, *"Drive-by" Jurisdiction: Congressional Oversight in Court*, 48 Pepperdine L. Rev. at 37, 44 (2020).

[44] Daniel Epstein, *The Illusory Precedent of McGrain v. Daugherty*, 3 UNT L. Rev. 1–9 (2021).

[45] McCubbins & Schwartz, *supra* note 17; McNollGast (1987), *supra* note 5 in Chapter 3.

[46] *Ohio Valley Water Co. v. Ben Avon*, 253 U.S. 287, 294 (1920).

[47] Epstein (2020), *supra* note 43.

bureaucracy does the oversight power arise (justified by Congress's rules of proceedings power) due to the need for Congress to monitor the implementation of its authority.[48] For instance, Congress oversees how Inspectors General investigate political officials and the administration of federal programs as well as oversees how the Securities and Exchange Commission investigates broker-dealers and investment advisers.

Independent of whether oversight should be narrowed in this way, my model expands upon current theories of delegation that do not address the incentives Congress has to delegate its investigative powers. These theories generally are unduly restrictive due to their limiting delegable legislative power to rulemaking. Because we can observe that Congress has increased the number of hearings held by committees and subcommittees with oversight jurisdiction while spending less time on any one hearing, I expect that Congress will delegate when doing so maximizes a preference for more hearings at less cost per hearing (what I call "oversight efficiency"). This informs my first hypothesis:

H1: Delegating investigative powers through the annual enactment of administrative subpoena statutes should increase oversight efficiency.

Delegation thus would be expected to increase Congress's ability to attain ideological gains if it enables Congress to reduce hearing costs while maximizing hearing returns. If delegating investigative power to the bureaucracy through administrative subpoena authority increases congressional oversight efficiency then the causal story would suggest that delegating subpoena powers reduces the need for Congress to directly police the private sphere. According to the Department of Justice, the most consistent user of administrative subpoenas is the Inspectors General.[49] Congress considers Inspectors General to be independent of political supervision by the executive agency and department heads yet the responsive agents of Congress.[50]

[48] John D. Huber & Charles R. Shipan, *Politics, Delegation, and Bureaucracy*, Oxford Handbook of Political Science (2011).

[49] U.S. Department of Justice, Report to Congress on the Use of Administrative Subpoena Authorities by executive branch Agencies and Entities, Pursuant to P.L. 106-55, Section 7, http://www.justice.gov/archive/olp/rpt_to_congress.htm (hereinafter "Department of Justice Report").

[50] *See e.g.*, U.S. Senate Committee on Environment and Public Works, Hearing Record on the Nomination of Robert Feitel for Inspector General of the Nuclear

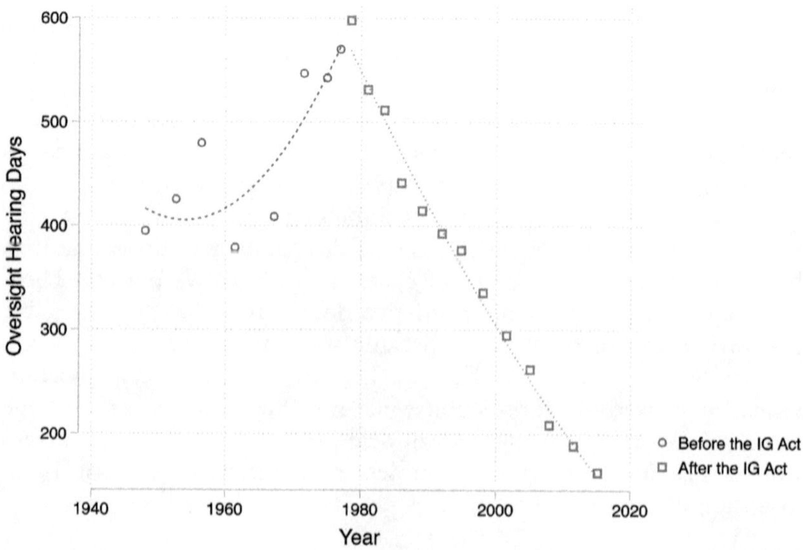

Fig. 3 Oversight hearing days before and after Inspector General Act passage

Figure 3 depicts the Fig. 2 trend of shorter oversight hearings as related to the 1978 enactment of the Inspector General Act (Fig. 4).

The question is whether this apparent pattern between the rise of Inspectors General and increasing oversight efficiency is causally related. As agencies increase their ability to investigate regulated parties both those agencies and the parties, whether through special interests or directly through reporting to Congress, are empowered to provide information to committees that shape Congress's oversight agenda. Likewise, if delegating impeachment (over officers) and rules of proceedings powers (over programs) to the bureaucracy through the creation of Inspectors General increases congressional oversight efficiency, then we can infer

Regulatory Commission (Dec. 3, 2019) at https://www.epw.senate.gov/public/_cache/files/a/0/a06b29ce-d4dd-4126-8d46-ac699542c2dc/C717626076D97D5D8A2EE7A9788DFAA4.spw-120319-nomination-hearing.pdf ("And if Mr. Feitel is confirmed, my colleagues in Congress and I will depend on him to keep us informed about the serious issues that may arise related to the NRC's program and to its operations."... "Senator Carper. Okay. How will you ensure that the work of the Office of Inspector General maintains its independence?"... "Senator Carper. One more. In your experience, what are the hallmarks of independent oversight that inspectors general are sworn to conduct?").

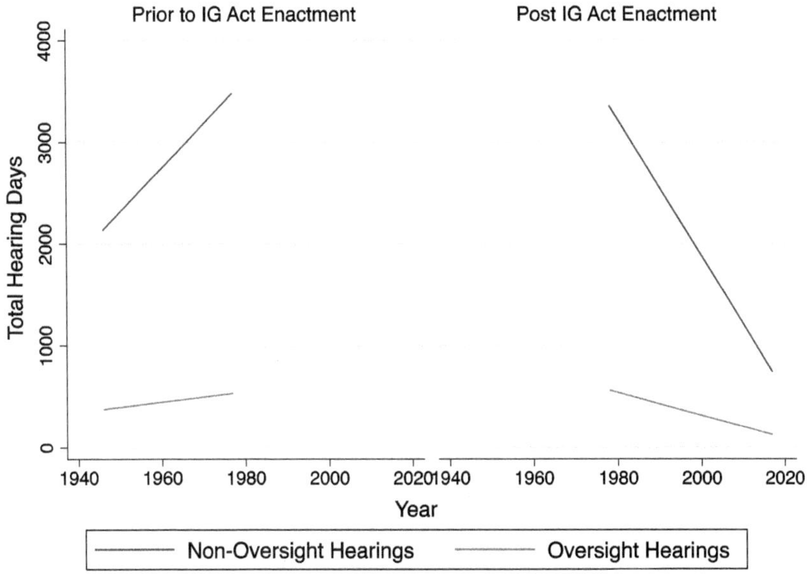

Fig. 4 Total annual hearing days (oversight versus non-oversight hearings) before and after Inspector General Act passage

that such delegation reduces the need for Congress to probe officials and programs directly. This informs the second hypothesis:

H2: Empowering Inspectors General with investigative authority should increase congressional oversight efficiency.

The first two hypotheses assume that maximizing the efficiency of oversight hearings maximizes electoral opportunities for members. By delegating its investigative burden to the agencies, Congress can reduce its own workload and maximize the resources it dedicates to translating investigative findings into political costs (or support) for the administration.

Given that Inspectors General annually issue the most administrative subpoenas by the federal government, I depict, in Fig. 5, the number of newly enacted statutory administrative subpoena authorizations from 1946 to 2020.

Figure 5 shows a spike in total new administrative subpoena-authorization statutes around 1978. This spike is caused, in substantial

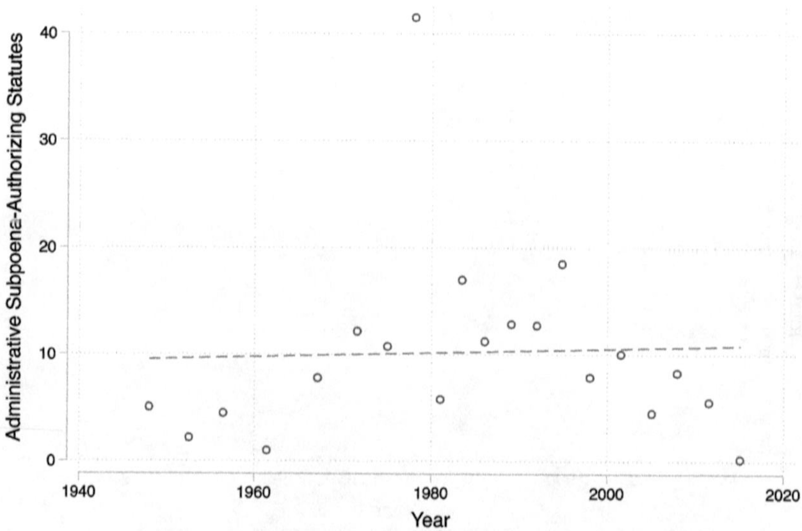

Fig. 5 Subpoena delegations per year (1946–2020)

part, by the fact that every cabinet-level Department was required to establish an Office of Inspector General authorized to compel compliance from the private sector with information requests via subpoena. Outside of this spike, the overwhelming majority of administrative subpoena authorities relate to the powers of certain departments and agencies to issue subpoenas to corporations in order to police violations of consumer protection, environmental, and social welfare statutes.

The findings of Inspectors General provided to Congress are different than the findings regulatory agencies, e.g., the Environmental Protection Agency (EPA) or FTC, present to Congress: Inspectors General provide information about waste, fraud, and abuse within a presidentially supervised Department whereas the EPA or FTC provides Congress with findings about violations of statutes by corporations and individuals. It therefore may be the case that the creation of departmental Inspectors General has unique and different effects on congressional oversight than the investigative activities of agencies and departments acting in a quasi-judicial, quasi-legislative role.

4.2 Bureaucratic Investigations as Law Enforcement

The president is the nation's chief law enforcement officer. As such, the assumption is that executive branch activity is, above anything else, law enforcement activity. In this sense, investigations by agencies would be thought to advance executive branch law enforcement interests.[51] While the early Supreme Court accepted the bureaucracy as a creature of legislative delegation and therefore understood regulatory investigations—subpoenas by the FTC or the Securities and Exchange Commission, for instance—to be legislative, not law enforcement,[52] the contemporary Supreme Court readily classifies administrative subpoenas as part and parcel of law enforcement.[53] Administrative subpoenas have been described as the 'backbone" of "regulatory enforcement."[54]

If the congressional authorization of administrative subpoena powers by the bureaucracy serves a law enforcement purpose, then why Congress would empower the bureaucracy with investigative powers given the theory that Congress establishes the bureaucracy and administrative procedures solely for purposes of controlling public policy. Oversight is theorized to be *ex post* delegation.

If Congress authorizes the bureaucracy to issue administrative subpoenas which permit greater law enforcement activities and this activity maximizes congressional oversight efficiency, then a number of inferences can be made. First, because granting administrative subpoena power to the bureaucracy permits greater law enforcement, administrative procedures here would actually decrease congressional control over policy by increasing bureaucratic discretion to enforce the law.[55] Second, congressional oversight would be theorized as less about bureaucratic control than, for instance, exposing executive branch activities that could

[51] Erin Murphy, *The Politics of Privacy in the Criminal Justice System: Information Disclosure, the Fourth Amendment, and Statutory Law Enforcement Exemptions*, 111 Mich. L. Rev. 485, 516 n. 136 (2013).

[52] *Oklahoma Press Publishing v. Walling*, 327 U.S. 186 (1946).

[53] *City of Los Angeles v. Patel*, 576 U.S. 409 (2015); *See v. Seattle*, 387 U.S. 541 (1967).

[54] Miriam H. Baer, *Law Enforcement's Lochner*, 105 Minn. L. Rev. 1667–1719 (2021).

[55] *United States v. Morton Salt*, 338 U.S. 632 (1950).

threaten the president and his party electorally.[56] Third, and most important, to the extent oversight involves the management of delegated power, Congress would be largely abdicating that responsibility and relying on law enforcement subpoenas and Inspector General investigations for ideologically salient findings.[57] The United States Department of Justice has increasingly relied upon administrative subpoenas for administrative, civil, and criminal enforcement.[58] Any mechanism where Congress relies on fire-alarm alerts of procedural violations by the bureaucracy to ensure control would suddenly be irrelevant. In short, such findings would suggest that Congress's preferred form of oversight is to hire (authorize) fire chiefs. The fire chiefs, protective of their independent discretionary power, will carry out the ideological preferences of the congressional majority by policing against infractions, empowering members with oversight authority to maximize their electoral goals. Hence the third hypothesis:

H3: Federal law enforcement activities should have no effect on congressional oversight efficiency.

[56] Theodora Galactos, *Note: The United States Department of Justice Environmental Crimes Section: A Case Study of Inter- and Intrabranch Conflict over Congressional Oversight and the Exercise of Prosecutorial Discretion*, 64 Fordham L. Rev. 587, 657 (1995) ("The more expansive the scope of congressional oversight activities, the greater the risk that an undisciplined representative could further party interests at the expense of law enforcement goals").

[57] *See e.g.*, 28 U.S.C. § 595I (1999, *expired*) ("An independent counsel shall advise the House of Representatives of any substantial and credible information which such independent counsel receives, in carrying out the independent counsel's responsibilities under this chapter, that may constitute grounds for an impeachment"); *accord*. Morrison v. Olson, 487 U.S. 654 (1988) (describing this provision as "congressional oversight").

[58] Department of Justice Report, *supra* note 49.

5 An Empirical Model of Delegation and Oversight

Consistent with prior scholarship on congressional oversight, I rely on congressional oversight hearings to measure oversight efficiency.[59] Congressional oversight hearings have consistently occurred since the middle of the nineteenth century. Even if variables like committee structure and staffing, oversight letters sent or reports drafted, or witness interviews or depositions conducted, would provide stronger measures of investigative activity by a given Congress, congressional oversight staffing ensures that investigative activity is valued to the extent that it culminates in a publicized televised hearing. I structure the data by individual hearing and year. Although I primarily rely upon the Policy Agendas Project dataset (derived from the Comparative Agendas Dataset), I hand-checked discrepancies in the data (caused by its coders relying on unofficial, third-party-generated Congressional Information Service abstracts[60]) against official hearing prints from the Government Printing Office and where I found inconsistencies, I conformed my data to the actual committee records. This strategy should not lead to changed empirical results so long as the identification of an oversight hearing is not based on keywords in the hearing title or transcript but on the identity of the relevant committee and subcommittee.

The Dependent Variable. Using data from the Comparative Agendas Dataset, I construct a dependent variable that measures the length, in days, of every congressional oversight hearing from 1946 to 2020 in both the House and the Senate. My data collection strategy differs from those of prior scholars who have sought to measure oversight through hearings by using keywords[61] or hearing content to classify a hearing as an oversight hearing. It also differs from those scholars who have sought to

[59] Dodd & Schott, *supra* note 11 at 156; Joel Aberbach, *Keeping a Watchful Eye: The Politics of Congressional Oversight*, 85–88 (1990); Keith Smith, *The Growth of Congressional Oversight*. Philadelphia, Annual Meeting of the American Political Science Association (2003); McGrath, *supra* note 2.

[60] The Congressional Information Service is now known as "Proquest Congressional".

[61] *See* McGrath (2013), *supra* note 2 at footnote 10 ("To be considered an oversight hearing, the Policy Agendas description must include at least one of the following keywords: oversight, review, report, budget request, control, impact, information, investigation, request, explanation, president, administration, contract, consultation, or examination.").

measure hearing duration.[62] These approaches ignore the cameral rules that define which committees and subcommittees have oversight jurisdiction. A House ethics committee hearing about an investigation that has nothing to do with the executive branch might be considered an oversight hearing under a content-based or keyword-based approach. Cameral rules, informed by the Rules of Proceedings clause, and clarified by the Legislative Reorganization Act of 1946, define an oversight hearing as a hearing by the House Oversight and Reform Committee, the Senate Committee on Homeland Security and Government Affairs, or by any oversight and investigations subcommittee.

The Legislative Reorganization Act of 1946 and its 1970 amendments established committees and subcommittees with permanent oversight responsibilities. The convention on Capitol Hill is to define any hearing by a committee or subcommittee with oversight jurisdiction as "oversight hearings" while other hearings are deemed "legislative hearings." This is especially the case given the Legislative Reorganization Act of 1946 and its amendments authorize the hiring of committee staff who, when hired by committees with oversight jurisdiction, do not have casework or bill-writing responsibilities. Under this identification strategy, I can measure the total number of oversight hearings over a time period like year or congressional term. Using the Policy Agendas codebook, I identify which committee and subcommittee codes captured standing oversight committees and subcommittees, identifying 19 such committees in the U.S. House of Representatives and 8 such committees in the U.S. Senate.[63] This identification strategy reveals that for these oversight hearings over time, the tendency is for hearing length, in days, to decrease as the number of hearings held per session increases. *See* Fig. 1 in Chapter 2

[62] *Id.*

[63] Using the Policy Agendas codebook, I could identify which committee and subcommittee codes captured standing oversight committees and subcommittees, identifying 19 such committees in the U.S. House of Representatives and 8 such committees in the U.S. Senate. On the House side, the committee with full oversight authority is House Oversight and Reform and the oversight subcommittees are House Agriculture, House Armed Services, House Commerce, House Education and Workforce, House Foreign Affairs, House Homeland Security, House Intelligence, House Natural Resources, House Science, House Small Business, House Transportation & Infrastructure, House Veterans Affairs, Senate Banking and Finance Oversight Hearings. On the Senate side, Homeland Security and Government Affairs is a full oversight committee and the relevant subcommittees with oversight jurisdiction are on the following committees: Senate Energy, and Senate Finance, Senate Health, Education, Labor & Pensions.

and Fig. 1. I infer from these trends a revealed preference concerning congressional oversight efficiency.

Alternative approaches to classifying a hearing as "oversight" based on hearing descriptions[64] tend to be biased by the activity of temporary select committees when compared to more permanent committees as well as lead to impractical outcomes like classifying only a portion of the hearings of the Committee on Oversight and Reform as actually being an oversight hearing. A better model accounts for the fact that any given oversight jurisdiction-holding committee hearing, even if it relates to legislation, *is* an oversight hearing. In replicating a keyword-based oversight hearing identification method,[65] I found that Policy Agendas hearing descriptions would often present quasi-investigative subject matters belied by the more mundane actual hearings when identified in the official government print. The Policy Agendas hearing descriptions are based on Congressional Information Service (CIS) abstracts which are not part of the official hearing record. Kriner and Schickler[66] (2014, 2016) distinguish between congressional "oversight" and investigations and code investigations by examining the Policy Agendas CIS hearing abstracts, handcoding these abstracts by conducting text analysis for investigative keywords. Scholars, relying on keywords from these secondary descriptions divorced from the primary record source, render their data collection prone to measurement error. Moreover, any method that overlooks the congressional choice to delegate the cameral oversight power to particular committees and subcommittees is susceptible to potential false positives for oversight identification, such as an appropriations committee hearing that examines Office of Management and Budget data collections that are described as investigations.

For committees with oversight jurisdiction, a hearing event is often a proxy for a staff-led congressional investigation. Measuring oversight in terms of hearing activities by committees with oversight jurisdiction will capture variation in the investigative activities of those committees' staff that would be ignored by a strategy of simply sampling hearings from all committees for investigative content. Consider that the House

[64] Smith, *supra* note 59; Kriner & Schickler, *Investigating the President: Congressional Checks on Presidential Power* (2016).

[65] McGrath, *supra* note 2; Kriner & Schickler, *supra* note 64.

[66] Kriner & Schickler, *id.*

Committee on Agriculture, subcommittee on Conservation and Forestry, could never enforce compulsory process nor contempt on grounds that an executive branch witness failed to comply with an investigative request. Yet coding hearings as "oversight" based on content would yield the unviable inference that a Conservation and Forestry subcommittee hearing could have predictive value concerning congressional control over the bureaucracy.

This coding strategy may also be underinclusive. Consider, for instance, that in March 1959, the House government expenditures committee (the predecessor to the House Oversight Committee) held a hearing on "US aid operations in Laos." This hearing was unmistakably an oversight hearing over the State Department but no coding scheme used by scholars to date identified this hearing as an oversight hearing. But coding hearings as "oversight" based on committee jurisdiction would not have missed this observation.

I am interested in identifying whether delegation of investigative authority to the bureaucracy influences oversight efficiency. My **key independent variable** is the total number of newly enacted administrative subpoena-authorizing statutes each year.

I propose that Congress's inserting language in statutes that authorize bureaucrats to issue administrative subpoenas is the key manner in which Congress delegates its investigative powers to governmental agents. Administrative subpoena authorizing statutes are uniquely suited to empirical work on congressional oversight and administrative law. Administrative subpoena statutes authorize agencies to subpoena regulated parties as part of administrative investigations to determine whether a statute is being complied with. As the Supreme Court recognized in *Oklahoma Press Publishing Company v. Walling*, administrative subpoenas are delegations by Congress of its compulsory power to obtain information necessary to regulate. Contemporary scholars have employed tools for measuring statute length or conducting text analysis as proxies for legislative delegations.[67] Studying administrative subpoena statutes presents a more direct way for political scientists to measure delegation for at least two reasons. First, when a statute says "the Secretary shall have the power to issue subpoenas" the statute is much more readily interpreted by the executive agency as delegating a specific power through a

[67] *See* note 3 in Chapter 3, and note 48 *supra*.

specific process versus, e.g., the Energy Policy Act's statement that "the Secretary shall make guarantees under this or any other Act for projects on such terms and conditions as the Secretary determines" which is where agencies exercise rulemaking or adjudicatory discretion.

Second, subpoena grants are much clearer evidence of intentional delegation by Congress than "as the Secretary determines" grants (typical of rulemaking). In other words, whether Congress delegates authority to an agency to issue a regulation or conduct a hearing, clear language is not necessary for an agency to exercise discretion, as the agency receives substantial deference to an interpretation needed to implement a policy command. However, in the case of subpoena grants, agencies are empowered with quasi-enforcement tools—a power to compel—and both Congress and the executive branch have incentives to ensure no uncertainty exists as to the interpretation of the delegation.[68]

As such, these statutes represent a pure form of delegation of legislative authority because there is no ambiguity as to how much discretion or power is delegated—once the agency has subpoena authority under some statute, it is authorized to compel information productions and enforce that compulsory process in court via the Department of Justice or some other organic act that permits independent litigating authority for noncompliance. There is no need for interpretive discretion by the agency.

Because Congress delegates subpoena authority each time an agency or a component within an agency is created, every enacted subpoena power is part of a larger statute establishing one or more regulatory norms. The reporting requirement in §7(a) of the presidential Threat Protection Act of 2000 required the U.S. Department of Justice to report to Congress on every legislative authorization of administrative subpoenas for use by the executive branch.[69] The Department of Justice data covered statutes on the books from the period of the early 1900s to 2001. In order to obtain data from after 2001, I conducted a *Lexis* search based upon the same

[68] *See* e.g., The Fair Labor Standards Act, 29 U.S.C. § 211(a) ("The Administrator or his designated representatives may investigate and gather data[]").

[69] Department of Justice Report, *supra* note 49. In this report, the Department of Justice explained the unique nature of administrative subpoenas as distinct from law enforcement due to such subpoenas not being subject to officer sworn warrant requirements nor part of a federal court-supervised process. As such, and consistent with *Humphrey's Executor*, these powers are non-executive.

key words used by the DOJ to report to Congress in order to extend the data.[70] Figure 4, shows that the number of statutory provisions delegating subpoena power has been fairly consistent over time.

One difficulty with measuring the effects of administrative subpoena authorizations is that a single statutory authorization may yield dozens of subpoenas from a single agency in a year. Relatedly, given the large numbers of subpoenas issued by the bureaucracy each year, congressional oversight committees are unlikely to be directly responsive to such subpoena activity even when subject to administrative procedures.

To evaluate how investigative delegations by Congress affect congressional oversight efficiency, I would ideally be able to observe all politically salient findings resulting from administrative subpoenas and requests for testimony or documents issued by federal agencies and agency Inspectors General in a given year. The difficulty is that these requests for information, responses, and conclusions are non-public and thus hard to measure. Further, a complex process exists where agency investigative outcomes are

[70] In order to build the independent variable counting the total number of new administrative subpoena-authorizing statutes per year, I was able to obtain all such organic (original source of given power) statutes from 1914 to 2001 from the U.S. Department of Justice's 2001 report to Congress pursuant to §7(a) of the presidential Threat Protection Act of 2000. The Justice Department data is highly reliable for several reasons: first, the Justice Department was required, by statute (P.L. 106-544, §7(a)), to conduct an executive branch-wide study on administrative subpoena authority, scope and protections; second, the Justice Department specifically demanded that all executive branch agencies and departments report to DOJ on their administrative subpoena authorities. I went through every statute identified and used LexisAdvance to code the date when the statute was first enacted with a subpoena authority. In order to obtain data since 2001, I built a search string in LexisAdvance for "subpoena, subpena (sic), Secretary AND 'collect data', 'study' AND 'Secretary', 'civil investigative demand', 'request information', 'investigate', 'request records', and 'request information'" and coded the dates of all statutes which clearly evinced the authorization of subpoena powers to an executive branch agency. It is important to note that the Inspector General Act of 1978 is only one statutory source but is the source for the overwhelming majority of the executive branch's issuance of administrative subpoenas per year. Although the Inspector General Act was amended in 1988, creating 30 designated federal entity Inspectors General authorized to subpoena under the 1978 Act, I coded the 1978 Act as 17, which were the original number of departments that from the single statute were mandated to create an Inspector General office and where that chief officer was granted administrative subpoena power. Interestingly, although the IG Act was passed during the second session of the 95th Congress, that session itself passed 37 independent administrative subpoena grants while the first session passed 7 such grants, which, excluding the IG Act, would still make the 95th Congress the single most aggressive subpoena authorizing Congress in the dataset.

translated—by the media, think tanks, or interest groups—into readily packaged content a committee staffer finds amenable for a hearing.

But here, legal doctrine informs the empirical model. The legal theory of oversight states that administrative subpoena powers are legislative in nature and delegated by Congress to the bureaucracy. The requirement that congressional subpoenas must be issued dependent upon a legislative purpose is suggestive of the expectation that administrative subpoenas would only affect congressional oversight as instrumented through agency rulemaking as a result of administrative investigations. This legal requirement, as applied to the bureaucracy, functions as an administrative procedure to ensure that agency investigations are appropriately legislative versus drift into law enforcement unreviewable by Congress.[71] In determining whether congressional delegation of investigative powers shapes congressional oversight, I therefore predict that congressional oversight efficiency is influenced by the effect of administrative subpoenas as instrumented through bureaucratic rulemaking.

To model this relationship, I identify all statutes that authorize regulatory investigations. Just as congressional subpoenas must be for the purpose of legislating, such legal rules concordantly govern the delegation of such subpoena power to the bureaucracy. A statute authorizing an agency to issue subpoenas will not directly affect congressional oversight activity. Nor is an administrative subpoena a final agency regulation. Instead, the actual subpoenas issued by the bureaucracy and the outcomes of those regulatory inquiries in terms of rules or orders will affect congressional oversight activity. The assumption is that Congress delegates policymaking to the bureaucracy and would not simply respond to agency investigations but to final policy decisions of the bureaucracy in the form of legislative rules. Administrative orders, which result from agency adjudications, apply to a single regulated party and are thus less likely than general rules issued from a public rulemaking process to affect Congress. My expectation is that as Congress authorizes the bureaucracy to increase its investigative activity, and those investigations inform legislative rules, Congress is able to avert any need to spend resources

[71] Congressional Oversight of the White House 45 Op. O.L.C. 1, 30 (Jan. 8, 2021) ("the law enforcement... privilege gives the executive branch a near-absolute right to withhold from Congress information that would compromise ongoing law enforcement activities").

conducting investigations in order to write policy.[72] Because the effects of delegation may not be immediate, I create a leading variable of the subsequent year's total oversight hearing length in order to examine how prior year subpoena authorizations affect legislative oversight efficiency.

Examining the effects of investigations on oversight efficiency as instrumented through bureaucratic regulation tests whether investigative delegations by Congress influence congressional willingness to spend resources conducting less but longer oversight hearings. The more investigative capacity granted to the bureaucracy, the less investigative legwork is borne on Congress in order to communicate newsworthy and politically salient findings through oversight hearings. It may also be the case that as congressional oversight committees are pressured to create politically useful hearing content, those committees become policy demanders of the bureaucracy, expecting useful content as compensation for empowering the bureaucracy. The alternative, or null, theory is that investigative delegations by Congress have no effect on congressional oversight efficiency. The null explanation would suggest that investigative delegation may be unrelated to institutional interests in oversight and that to the extent agenda-setting reduced congressional oversight efficiency, committees and their staff would have a more meaningful causal role.[73] Alternatively, it may be the case that administrative subpoenas do not inform rulemaking but law enforcement. Under this alternative hypothesis, statutory subpoena authorities empower the bureaucracy to advance executive branch law enforcement interests exempt from constitutional procedures arising from the Fourth and Fifth amendments. Evidence that administrative subpoenas lead to enforcement outcomes—rather than rulemaking—would be evidence that would counter the oversight-delegation theory.

[72] Aberbach, *supra* note 59.

[73] Under House Rule X, Clause 2(d)(2), all House committee oversight plans are submitted to the Chair of the House Oversight Committee. *See* Oversight Plans for all House Committees, House Report 114-82 (114th Cong., 1st Sess.) (Apr. 15, 2015), *available at* https://www.congress.gov/114/crpt/hrpt82/CRPT-114hrpt82.pdf. One such oversight plan topic states, "[i]n February 2015, the Government Accountability Office will issue its biannual High Risk report, which identifies government programs that are particularly vulnerable to waste, fraud, and abuse. The Committee will provide ongoing oversight of agencies and programs included on the High Risk list by holding hearings, meeting with agency officials responsible for included programs, and monitoring agencies' corrective plans and actions'").

Other Independent Variables. To measure rulemaking, I develop a year-by-year measure of page counts from the Code of Federal Regulations. I used George Washington University Regulatory Studies Center data to code the total length of the Code of Federal Regulations (CFR) by pages per year. I avoid simply a count of each independent and newly added regulation for each yearly Unified Agenda because such a metric would need to be weighted by previously added regulations that are still in effect as well as previously rescinded regulations whereas a page count is a continuous variable that reflects all currently in-effect regulations.

Entities that issue administrative subpoenas—independent agencies, GAO, or Inspectors General—are statutorily required to report their findings to Congress, independent of whether they had to use a subpoena to get the information.[74] Of those findings, I expect that only the most politically salient ones are incorporated into the oversight hearing agenda by congressional committees. The IG Act created permanent audit and investigative officers in every federal department. After the Inspector General Act's passage, federal officers were empowered to police waste, fraud, and abuse in all federal agencies, thus presenting Congress with a direct source of information for setting its oversight agenda as well as reducing Congress's previous investigative workload.

Whenever an Inspector General decides to go public with a proposed investigation, to release an audit or investigative report, or to inform Congress about activities it has the discretion to keep confidential, the signal immediately influences Congress's oversight agenda, whether to signal what to look at or what issue is already saturated. Delegation of congressional investigative power to Inspectors General allows Congress to delegate oversight to federal officials in order to increase the amount of information available to it in order to exercise political control.[75]

Because Inspectors General engage in the overwhelming majority of administrative subpoena activity each year and I suspect that Inspectors General engage in oversight agenda-setting, I include a dummy variable distinguishing between hearings before and after the passage of the Inspector General Act.

[74] 5 U.S.C. Appx. § 5.

[75] David Epstein & Sharyn O'Halloran, *A Theory of Strategic Oversight: Congress, Lobbyists, and the Bureaucracy*, 11 J. L., Econ. & Org. (1995) at 227–255.

I also include the total number of hearings per year and the total number of oversight hearings per year to control for the possibility that oversight hearing length is simply an effect of the incidence of hearings. Finally, I include variables coding each hearing in terms of the political party in control of the House, Senate, and White House at the time to control for the possibility that observed effects are primarily caused by a divided government.

Finally, in order to test the alternative hypothesis styled as Hypothesis 3, that oversight efficiency should not be affected by congressional authorization of more investigative discretion for law enforcement activity through administrative subpoena authorizations, I obtain criminal filings from the Department of Justice for all available years in which information is made available.

I predict the delegation of investigative powers reduces the length of oversight hearings, thus allowing Congress to maximize its capacity to increase the number of congressional oversight hearings held per year. This prediction assumes that Congress increases hearing activity (hearings are efficient ways to gain publicity and credit-claiming opportunities) in response to delegation, which confirms the belief of the congressional framers of the Legislative Reorganization Act that oversight is largely a reaction to modern administration.

6 Results

To test Hypothesis 1, I regress administrative subpoena authorizations per year as instrumented through rulemaking (total page count per Congress in the Code of Federal Regulation) and the total number of oversight hearings against the dependent variable of the length of oversight hearings. I also model control variables including gridlock scores, identification of the party in control of each house of Congress and the White House ("1" for Democratic, "0" for Republican), as well as the indicator variable for whether ("1") or not ("0") the Inspector General Act was enacted into law. Because the number of oversight hearings per year are totals of events, we can conceive of them as count outcomes appropriate for Poisson regression (Table 1).

I do not find statistical support for inferring that administrative subpoena activity affects oversight efficiency when instrumented through rulemaking. When I include the indicator variable identifying hearings in terms of their incidence before or after the Inspector General Act's

Table 1 Effects of delegating investigative powers on oversight efficiency (1946–2020)

	(1) Instrumental variable model (administrative subpoenas affecting hearings through rules)	*(2) Instrumental variable model (administrative subpoenas affecting hearings through rules)*	*(3) Instrumental variable model (administrative subpoenas affecting hearings through rules)*
	Total oversight hearing days per year (leading indicator)	*Total oversight hearing days per year (leading indicator)*	*Total oversight hearing days per year (leading indicator)*
Bureaucratic investigations instrumented through rules	0.000	0.000	0.000
	(0.000)	(0.000)	(0.000)
Total oversight hearings (per year)	−0.013	−0.002	−0.005
	(0.007)	(0.003)	(0.008)
Pre v. Post IG Act		−0.831*	−1.171
		(0.383)	(0.920)
Party identification of the president			−0.0814
			(0.137)
Senate Party identification			−0.706
			(0.5892)
House Party identification			0.801*
			(0.398)
Constant	6.131***	5.949***	5.937***
	(0.479)	(0.158)	(0.359)
Observations	70	70	70

Standard errors in parentheses
$^{*}p < 0.05$, $^{**}p < 0.01$, $^{***}p < 0.001$

passage, I observe that as the likelihood that an oversight hearing occurred after passage of the Inspector General Act increases, the length of hearing days in a year increases by 0.44 (natural exponent of –0.831) days. This result provides a non-substantive basis for rejecting Hypothesis 2 concerning the Inspectors General as increasing legislative oversight efficiency. As the other independent variables are added into the model, the Inspector General Act indicator variable loses its significance even as Democratic Party control of the House of Representatives tends to increase the total number of annual oversight hearing days by 2.22 (natural exponent of 0.801).

The models in Table 1 (and Figs. 12 and 13 in Appendix C) raise questions as to the different effects of the Inspector General Act and increases in congressional investigative authorizations. The power of Inspectors General to investigate at any point after the statutory enactment in 1978 does not depend upon reauthorization or additional statutory authorities—a single statute enables a limitless number of possible inquiries. The next model explores the independent causal effects on hearing length resulting from the Inspector General Act.

Given the graphical representations in Figs. 2 and 4 and the leverage of the delegation of oversight power as a modeling tool, I test Hypothesis 2 by constructing a difference-in-differences model that examines the effects of the Inspector General Act of 1978 (95th Congress) on the duration for a given oversight hearing. The difference-in-differences model is appropriate when none of the observations are subject to treatment in the pre-treatment period and where we would not expect treatment to have an effect on the outcome for observations that were not subject to treatment. It is certainly plausible to imagine that members' choice to reduce oversight hearing length is not conditioned upon the existence of an Inspector General. In the absence of treatment, the average outcomes for the treated (congressional oversight hearings) should have the same variation over time as the average outcomes for the control (non-oversight hearings).[76] It is also plausible that the treatment of the Inspector General Act is exogenous to the data, i.e., the likelihood of treatment being a result of post-Nixon bureaucratic reforms versus, e.g., the Legislative Reorganization Act of 1970. Finally, the passage of the

[76] James Heckman et al., *Characterizing Selection Bias Using Experimental Data*, 66 Econometrica (1998), 1017–1098; Adam Glynn & Konstantin Kashin, *Front-Door Difference-in-Differences Estimators*, 61 Am. J. Pol. Sci. (2017), 989–1002.

Inspector General Act is expected to have an immediate effect on the structure of oversight.

I hypothesize that the passage of the Inspector General (IG) Act in 1978, which led to an immediate spike of statutory sources for federal administrative subpoena powers, has an as-if random effect, if it has any, on congressional oversight hearing days. Because Inspectors General can be relied upon as a consistent, though unpredictable, source of information and because a single act of Congress (in 1978) provides a continuing authorization for Cabinet-level Department monitoring, Inspector General activity can be conceived of as an exogenous activity that both influences subsequent congressional oversight but also reduces the need for Congress to exercise resources to obtain information.

Indeed, the political expectation that Inspectors General are politically independent means that their activities must be insulated from congressional control. It is important to note, however, that Inspectors General existed prior to the 1978 Inspector General Act's passage yet had authority restricted to the organic statutes of their respective agencies rather than a shared authority based in Title 5. These Inspectors General were not appointed by the president, not given the set of powers made clear in 1978, nor consistently present throughout the executive branch. Second, these latter circumstances explain an additional confounder: the timing of the Inspector General Act overlaps with a significant number of post-Nixon civil service reforms including the Ethics in Government Act, the Civil Service Reform Act, and the Presidential Records Act. Any effects observed in a model may be caused by another executive branch-accountability statute or by the fact that 1978 was a year that itself signaled a shift in congressional oversight of the executive. As a general comment, evidence of such large shifts would nevertheless be suggestive of the institutional effects of Congress using statutes to regulate executive branch discretion. More specifically, there are unique reasons to expect independent effects from the Inspector General Act. Unlike the Ethics in Government Act or record keeping laws, which are ultimately enforced by the Attorney General, the Inspector Generals have independent enforcement authority.

There are other intuitive reasons to view Inspector General investigations as as-if random when applied to Congress's oversight hearing days. When it comes to policing federal agency conduct, no administrative procedures permit an interested party to obtain judicial review of Inspector General decision-making. There is no private right to force an Inspector General to investigate a matter. Because Inspectors General make referrals to law enforcement agencies, they can rely on executive and other enforcement privileges to conceal their activities from disclosure to Congress or the public as well as block judicial review of agency actions connected to Inspector General involvement in an ongoing investigation.

This fact also presents an as-if random treatment condition: because Congress empowered Inspectors General as independent, the investigative agenda of an Inspector General is self-determined and confidential and Congress has an incentive to protect the integrity and objectivity of the Inspector General process when investigative findings present the opportunity for credit-claiming. While Congress, particularly oversight chairs, may request audits or investigations by Inspectors General and while affected members of the public can report waste, fraud, or abuse to Offices of Inspectors General, the Inspectors General are free to ignore congressional and public requests. Departmental Inspectors General are nominated by the president and confirmed by the Senate and lack term limits.

As further evidence of Inspector General independence, the traditional controls of executive branch agents—such as congressional appropriations or presidential removal—presents political obstacles to Congress and the president, for cutting appropriations to or removing a watchdog would run counter to precisely that ideological incentive (or unobserved factor signaling its weight) motivating a Member to engage in oversight and an Inspector General, by statutory design, can only be removed by the president with prior notice to Congress. Thus, the president is deterred by political censure if he or she tries to use the removal power to control an Inspector General's agenda.

Even if the same unobserved covariates that predict congressional oversight hearing days were to significantly predict Inspector General activity, as applied to Congress, the Inspector General's activities are unpredictable and quasi-random. At a minimum, the introduction of Inspectors General would have no direct effect on hearing days but would instead influence variation in other congressional oversight activities, like the investigative agenda of the staff, which may influence the length of oversight hearing days.

As the results in Table 2 show, the differences in oversight hearing days before and after the Inspector General Act's passage are significant, and the IG Act's effects cause the significant differences between oversight hearings and non-oversight hearings before Inspector General Act enactment and as affected after enactment. When substituting the total number of hearings for the duration as the dependent variable (Model 4), we observe that while prior to the Inspector General Act, Congress held more non-oversight hearings than oversight hearings, after the passage of the Inspector General Act, Congress held more oversight hearings than non-oversight hearings, with the difference between differences reflecting a net average increase in 205.3 oversight hearings after Inspector General Act passage. Inspectors General, as fire chiefs who fuel the congressional oversight agenda, enable Congress to increase the number of oversight hearings it conducts while reducing the length of time a given hearing costs. The promise of the Legislative Reorganization Act—that Congress would police waste, fraud, and abuse in federal programs—has largely been met by a strategic delegation of "continuous watchfulness" to the Inspectors General.

These results show that delegating congressional investigative authority over businesses to the bureaucracy does not enable more oversight efficiency. Congress prefers a method of oversight that maximizes publicity while minimizing investigative workload. While the initial hypothesis (H1) conceives of the rational oversight member seeking to maximize the number of and minimize the length of each hearing, the support for the second hypothesis (H2) reflects that Congress maximizes its oversight efficiency in delegating its investigative powers over bureaucratic policy versus its investigative powers over businesses. The Inspectors General conduct the heavy investigative lifting leaving Congress with a more efficient mechanism for claiming credit and taking positions over the investigative findings.

That delegation of investigative authority to Inspectors General seems to increase congressional oversight efficiency while delegation to agencies via legally enforceable investigations and rulemaking has no statistically significant effects on efficiency, reveals another distinction within the Inspector General Act. While Inspectors General have substantial subpoena authority over businesses receiving federal funds, Inspectors General are statutorily required to not use subpoenas when conducting investigations of federal employees. Congress's establishing an administrative procedure limiting Inspectors General from using their administrative subpoena powers to investigate the bureaucracy increases congressional oversight efficiency.

But this finding leads to another issue: if Congress does not increase its oversight efficiency by delegating its power to investigate the private

Table 2 Difference-in-differences models on the effects of the establishment of Departmental Inspectors General on oversight efficiency

	(1) Hearing length (in days)	(2) Hearing length (in days) w/ covariates	(3) Total hearing days	(4) Total hearings
Effects of IG Act on untreated (non-oversight hearings)	−1.044***	−0.807***	−762.9***	180.6***
	(0.0151)	(0.0304)	(6.340)	(3.209)
Difference between oversight and non-oversight hearings pre IG Act	2.318***	2.315***	50.77**	−81.41***
	(0.0426)	(0.0424)	(17.95)	(9.084)
Difference-in-differences estimate of the treatment effect	**−1.664***	**−1.617***	**−190.1***	**205.3***
	(0.0515)	(0.0513)	(21.63)	(10.95)
Total agency rules		−0.00000187***		
		(0.000000285)		
Administrative subpoena-authorizing statutes		0.00233***		
		(0.000678)		
House Party identification		0.514***		
		(0.0217)		
Senate Party identification		−0.189***		
		(0.0196)		
Party identification of the president		0.131***		
		(0.0152)		
Constant	2.491***	2.216***	2.491***	629.5***
	(0.0118)	(0.0248)	(0.0118)	(2.525)
Observations	98,950	98,950	98,950	100,254

Standard errors in parentheses
*$p < 0.05$, **$p < 0.01$, ***$p < 0.001$

sector, it may be the case that Inspectors General and bureaucrats are using their administrative subpoena authority not to make policy but to increase federal law enforcement capacity. Delegation of Congress's investigative power over corporations—itself a key, yet overlooked power of Congress—to independent enforcement agencies like Federal Trade

Commission as well as the OIGs versus delegation of congressional investigations of agency programs to OIGs have differing effects on oversight efficiency; for oversight committees, findings of corporate misconduct may force members to spend more time on hearings with low ideological gains whereas findings of programmatic misconduct enhance congressional incentives for oversight. But if the congressional delegation of the power to investigate the private sphere does not directly enhance oversight efficiency and instead enhances federal law enforcement power, such delegation functions as increased law enforcement discretion to the executive branch.

Because such a possibility would mean grants of subpoena authorities are executive powers wielded by executive officers, Hypothesis 3 proposes that federal law enforcement activities should have no effect on oversight efficiency. In other words, Congress's *legislative* power to investigate business conduct and enforce subpoenas in court, when granted to the bureaucracy in the form of administrative subpoenas, should affect congressional oversight efficiency, if at all, through bureaucratic legislation (rules). But if Congress's authorizing the bureaucracy to use *legislative* power to engage in law enforcement increases oversight efficiency, then the findings in the Table 1 model would suggest that Congress is not delegating its investigative powers to the bureaucracy but instead authorizing the executive branch with legislative power for law enforcement, not policy, purposes. To test this possibility, I add the data on federal criminal filings to the Table 1 models.

Administrative subpoenas, also known as civil investigative demands, from OIGs and agencies like the Federal Trade Commission, Securities and Exchange Commission, National Labor Relations Board, Commodities Futures Trading Commission, Food and Drug Administration, Federal Communications Commission, and Consumer Product Safety Commission are commonly used to form the basis for criminal enforcement actions.[77] Congress is more likely to respond to decisions to file criminal cases underlying subpoena-obtained information than it would to decisions to bring administrative or civil cases. First, while the executive branch can enforce the laws administratively and civilly, administrative enforcement is often only publicized through a final decision and order when an administrative complaint proves successful. The public

[77] Department of Justice Report, *supra* note 49.

filing of criminal cases is independent of the outcomes of those enforcement matters. Second, the political leadership of the executive branch, typically the U.S. Department of Justice, does not have oversight over administrative enforcement by boards and commissions but does exercise prosecutorial discretion as to law enforcement referrals from agencies and Inspectors General. Third, because congressional enactment of civil enforcement authority evolved over the time period examined (1946–2020), we cannot assume that each filing in the sample is independent of and equally distributed as any other filing and thus civil filing data is likely skewed.[78] Finally, criminal enforcement filings are often based on referrals where prosecutorial discretion is independent of the decision to proceed administratively and civilly, yet solely pursuing civil enforcement often means that a decision was made not to pursue a matter criminally, thus further leading to bias in estimates based on civil filings. I display the results of these models in Table 3.

The results in the first two models of Table 3 show that federal criminal filings have substantively small but statistically significant increases in congressional oversight efficiency both when considering the effects of investigative delegations and rulemaking to be separate as well as considering investigative delegations to only affect oversight through rules. Note, however, that when exponentiating such small values, whether negative or positive, the substantive effect is approximately the same. Appendix D shows that the effects of federal criminal filings remain substantively insignificant even when considering the effects on a given hearing. The effect of federal criminal filings is only not statistically significant when political factors like party control are included in the model (which also makes the Inspector General Act indicator variable non-significant). Given political factors, including the Inspector General Act indicator, mute the effects of federal criminal filings on oversight efficiency suggest that such factors have poor explanatory value when examining how law enforcement affects oversight.

[78] *See* Judiciary Act of 1789, § 9, 1 Stat. 73 (granting federal courts jurisdiction exclusive of the states over "all crimes and offenses... cognizable under the authority of the United States" but granting the federal courts concurrent jurisdiction with the states over "all suits at common law where the United States sue[.]").

Table 3 Effects of law enforcement on oversight efficiency (1946–2020)

	(1) Negative binomial regression	*(2) Instrumental variable model (administrative subpoenas affecting hearings through rules)*	*(3) Instrumental variable model (administrative subpoenas affecting hearings through rules)*
	Total oversight hearing days per year (leading indicator)	*Total oversight hearing days per year (leading indicator)*	*Total oversight hearing days per year (leading indicator)*
Total number of oversight hearings (per year)	0.003**	−0.008*	−0.005
	(0.001)	(0.004)	(0.01)
Federal criminal cases filed (per year)	−0.000*	−0.000*	−0.000
	(0.000)	(0.000)	(0.000)
Total agency rules	−0.000**	0.000*	0.000
	(0.000)	(0.000)	(0.000)
Administrative subpoena-authorizing statutes	0.01***		
	(0.003)		
Party identification of the president			−0.384
			(0.41)
Senate Party identification			−0.254
			(0.255)
House Party identification			0.397***
			(0.119)
Pre v. Post IG Act			−1.22
			(1.07)

(continued)

Table 3 (continued)

	(1) Negative binomial regression	*(2) Instrumental variable model (administrative subpoenas affecting hearings through rules)*	*(3) Instrumental variable model (administrative subpoenas affecting hearings through rules)*
	Total oversight hearing days per year (leading indicator)	*Total oversight hearing days per year (leading indicator)*	*Total oversight hearing days per year (leading indicator)*
Constant	6.144*** (0.115)	6.613*** (0.191)	6.147*** (0.826)
/			
lnalpha	−2.754*** (0.166)		
Observations	70	70	70
Adjusted R^2			

Standard errors in parentheses
$^{*}p < 0.05$, $^{**}p < 0.01$, $^{***}p < 0.001$

7 Discussion

Does the delegation of investigatory powers shape congressional oversight? The results suggest that the answer depends upon *which* investigatory powers. Congress has the power to compel information from the private sphere for the purpose of crafting legislative policy, it has the ability to request information from the bureaucracy to inform the public on regulatory policies and programs, and, finally, it has the ability to investigate the president and her copartisans in view of possible impeachment. The results show that Congress can oversee the bureaucracy and score points against an administration by delegating legislative power to the Inspectors General. When it comes to Office of Inspector General investigations of federal programs and the employees involved in them, the Inspectors General allow Congress to reduce its workload and maximize ideological gains when oversight committees go public with Inspectors General findings. Moreover, the fact that Inspectors General are responsive to congressional requests and sensitive to the electoral risk facing a president who decides to remove an Inspector General indicates that the Inspector General Act's administrative procedures, most importantly mandatory reporting to Congress,[79] is effective in increasing legislative control over the bureaucracy while minimizing presidential control.[80]

So why does subpoena delegation in the form of the Inspector General Act lead to different results than the continuous subpoena delegations over time shown in the regression analysis in Table 1? One possibility is that administrative subpoena authorizations directed outside Inspector General offices only affect Congress through agency rulemaking activity whereas Inspector General subpoenas are unconnected to bureaucratic policymaking in the form of rules. Before the passage of the Inspector General Act, the average oversight hearing would last 4.8 days (with the average length of a non-oversight hearing being 2.5 days); after the passage of the Inspector General Act, the average length of an oversight hearing drops to 2.1 days (with the average non-oversight hearing lasting 1.5 days).

As the additional models in Appendix C show, adding in placebos in 1970[81] and 1988[82] to determine whether the 1978 Inspector General Act uniquely affects oversight efficiency shows that such alternative models would violate the parallel trends assumption required for causal effects in the difference-in-differences model. The Inspector General offices affected by the model are restricted to cabinet-level departments whereas the entire bureaucracy, including independent agencies, can exercise administrative subpoena power. The difference between a model that treats all subpoena delegations equally and one that restricts effects to the Inspector General Act tells us something about oversight of cabinet departments (which presidentially appointed Inspectors General oversee) versus oversight over independent enforcement agencies (which are investigating regulated businesses and whose Inspectors General are appointed by the agency, not the president). While statutes that empower agencies to issue legislative rules with the force of law tend to be one-shot

[79] 5 U.S.C. Appx. § 5(a).

[80] Section 5(e) of the Inspector General acts authorizes any member of Congress to obtain information from an Inspector General notwithstanding the President's decision to keep such information secret.

[81] Representing the 1970 Legislative Reorganization Act.

[82] In 1988, the Inspector General Act was amended to create Inspectors General at non-cabinet agencies and commissions. However, these Inspectors General are not appointed by the President and confirmed by the Senate but are appointed by the agency head (called "designated federal entity" IGs).

deals—in the sense that an agency may issue and subsequently revise a rule based upon a statute rather than crafting several rules from one statute—investigative delegations empower agencies to issue countless subpoenas from a single legal authority. Because the sorts of preliminary investigative findings resulting from administrative subpoenas might require more resource investment by committee staff than final enforcement actions or the findings of Inspectors General from investigations of the bureaucracy, Congress may lack the capacity to oversee quasi-legislative administrative investigations. One implication is that if Congress delegates without oversight, it has abdicated authority, and thus the once-delegated power becomes an executive power subject to the discretion of the executive.

These results should make scholars suspicious of the status of Inspectors General as presidential appointees who serve at the pleasure of the president given the causal effects of Inspectors General on oversight strongly supports the prediction that Congress delegates its oversight over the bureaucracy to Inspectors General who are serving Congress, not the president, as the *de facto* principal. These results also show how congressional oversight practices change over time to advance the electoral interests of members: by delegating legislative power to and establishing legislative officers within the executive branch, Congress can increase the number of hearings held at less duration per hearing. That Congress can increase its oversight efficiency by creating presidentially appointed officers (fire chiefs) indicates a powerful legislative principal.

Concerning the legislative power to investigate businesses, congressional enactment of administrative subpoena powers increases congressional oversight efficiency at a statistically significant level, but not through the creation of administrative procedures via delegation. The legislative power to investigate the private sector is how modern legislatures revise or reform business regulations to support the general welfare. If neither Congress nor the bureaucracy uses that power of regulatory investigations to inform legislative rules, an essential aspect of modern policymaking is disregarded. The results suggest that Congress is able to maximize its electoral interests—albeit at a substantively negligible impact—by authorizing the executive branch to utilize legislative powers for law enforcement, not policy, purposes.[83] Certainly, delegation implies

[83] *See* U.S. Department of Justice, Justice Manual, § 1997 ("The Attorney General has delegated authority to issue administrative subpoenas to the United States Attorneys, the Assistant Attorney General of the Criminal Division and the Director of the FBI, with

that Congress has the power to engage in the delegated act itself and Congress lacks any law enforcement power. Because political factors like party control, or policy factors like rulemaking, do not influence the effects of law enforcement filings, the findings from Tables 1 and 3 show that Congress's oversight strategy, to the extent it exists, concerning the private sector does not rely on administrative procedures for maintaining political control as part of the advancement of a policy agenda.

8 Conclusion

This chapter provides empirical support for the theory that Congress delegates its investigative powers to the executive branch in a similar fashion to its delegation of legislative powers (rulemaking) and that such delegations influence how Congress structures its oversight activities. What this theory says about the study of congressional oversight of the bureaucracy supports the fire-alarm theory with an additional understanding of its features: Congress prefers to delegate policing to police officers. To continue the McNollGast analogy, Congress would rather hire a police or fire chief than respond to fire alarms or engage in police patrolling itself. The hypotheses tested in this chapter provide substantial support for the maxim that Congress will only establish administrative procedures governing its delegation of its investigative powers of bureaucratic monitoring, political inquiries, and regulatory investigations if such procedures maximize the electoral rewards made possible by "oversight efficiency": more (publicity), shorter (workload) hearings. I find support that the creation of departmental Inspectors General increased congressional oversight efficiency by allowing Congress to more efficiently allocate oversight resources: more hearings with less total time spent on hearings.

The findings challenge key assumptions in the political science and legal literatures. American constitutional jurisprudence has supposed that a congressional oversight request "is valid only if it is 'related to, and in furtherance of, a legitimate task of the Congress,'" it "must serve a 'valid legislative purpose.'"[84] Further, "the scope of oversight authority

the power to redelegate to AUSAs, FBI Special Agents in charge and Senior Supervisory Resident Agents, and Criminal Division Trial Attorneys.").

[84] *Trump v. Mazars USA, LLP*, 140 S. Ct. 2019, 2031 (2020) (quoting *Watkins*, 354 U.S. at 187; *Quinn v. United States*, 349 U.S. 155, 161 (1955)).

is limited to subjects 'on which legislation could be had,' and therefore Congress 'cannot inquire into matters which are within the exclusive province of one of the other branches of the Government,' including any function committed exclusively to the president by the Constitution."[85]

Notwithstanding that the precedent, in *McGrain v. Daugherty*, concerning "legislative purpose" requirements was limited solely to congressional investigations of the private sector,[86] the fact that Inspectors General make findings which can support presidential impeachment reflects the real sense in which oversight extends beyond subjects "on which legislation could be had." And while political scientists conceptualize bureaucratic oversight as political control to prevent policy drift, two crucial aspects of Congress's investigative powers—investigations of political officials and the private sector—both of which can be and are tasked to the executive branch itself, are not themselves monitored for purposes of creating or modifying public policy as much as to ensure bureaucratic agents are effectively identifying infractions that can help Congress advance the electoral interests of its members.

In the last few years, Congress has more aggressively empowered officials like the Comptroller General, the Special Counsel, and the several Inspectors General to access information the executive power-zealous Office of Legal Counsel has viewed as protected under executive branch confidentiality interests, e.g., access to Grand Jury materials, consumer information, wiretap information, attorney–client communications or deliberative communications.[87] In 2016, Congress passed and the president signed the Inspector General Empowerment Act of 2016, which overturned Office of Legal Counsel legal decisions concerning the application of civil discovery privileges against Inspectors General by

[85] Memorandum Opinion for the Counsel to the President, *Congressional Oversight of the White House*, 45 Op. O.L.C. 1, 10 (Jan. 8, 2021) (internal citations omitted).

[86] Daniel Epstein, *The Illusory Precedent of McGrain v. Daugherty*, 4 UNT Dall. L. Rev. 1–9 (2021) (originally published at 38 Yale J. Reg. Notice and Comment (2020)).

[87] *See e.g., The Department of Justice Inspector General's Access to Information Protected by the Federal Wiretap Act, Rule 6(e) of the Federal Rules of Criminal Procedure, and Section 626 of the Fair Credit Reporting Act*, 39 Slip. Op. O.L.C. at 1–67 (July 20, 2015), *available at* https://www.justice.gov/sites/default/files/olc/opinions/attachments/2017/01/17/2015-07-20-doj-oig-access-ed-note.pdf.

granting Inspectors General access to "all" records, reports and documents "notwithstanding any other provision of law".[88] In 2017, Congress reauthorized the Office of Special Counsel and amended the statute to provide the Special Counsel "timely access" to "all" records, reports, and documents where "[a] claim of common law privilege ... shall not prevent to Special Counsel from obtaining" the material.[89] On January 21, 2017, the GAO Access and Oversight Act of 2017 became law, which for the first time authorized the Comptroller General to bring "civil actions" to "obtain such agency records as the Comptroller General requires to discharge the duties of the Comptroller General[.]"[90] It is difficult to describe these laws as other than congressional delegations of power lacking intelligible limiting principles.

Concerning legislative inquiries over the private sector, this is an area where Congress has traditionally stood on strong legal grounds to rely on the courts to enforce subpoenas for information and documents. Congressional delegation of this power to the bureaucracy would be possible if subpoenas were subject to the legislative requirement that the investigation be for a legitimate lawmaking purpose. In the context of the bureaucracy, this requirement takes the form of administrative procedures to ensure that administrative subpoenas are for a legitimate rulemaking purpose. The results show that administrative subpoena activity does not directly or indirectly when instrumented through rules, enhance congressional oversight efficiency. Instead, when administrative subpoena authorities are understood not as legislative delegations subject to legislative control but as authorizations subject to executive branch law enforcement discretion, some evidence of salutary effects of law enforcement on oversight efficiency exists. While Inspectors General are limited to non-enforcement inquiries to the bureaucracy, according to the U.S. Department of Justice "Inspector General [subpoena] authority is mainly used in criminal investigations."[91] While it is difficult to measure how Inspector General reports to Congress on bureaucratic infractions uniquely affect Congress in ways that criminal filings based on Inspector General investigations do not, the evidence raises the specter

[88] 5 U.S.C. app. § 6(a)(1)(A), (B).

[89] 5 U.S.C. § 1212(b) (2017).

[90] 31 U.S.C. § 716(b).

[91] Department of Justice Report, *supra* note 49.

that Congress best ensures executive branch policy coheres with its own policy preferences through administrative procedures that apply to all agencies and are delimited by jurisdictional constraints.

The empirical results in this chapter also suggest how both legal and political theories of congressional oversight are unduly narrow. The Supreme Court's *Oklahoma Press Publishing* and *Morton Salt* decisions, conceiving of administrative subpoenas as legislative in nature, may no longer meaningfully refer to the structure of American politics today. While bureaucratic subpoena activities may have been subject to legislative control up until shortly after 1946, today such statutes serve as executive branch law enforcement authorizations. As such, how the bureaucracy conducts investigations of the private sector is not subject to congressional control. This inference comports with political intuitions about oversight of the bureaucracy: congressional hearings focus on an administration's political failures, not the policies advanced in agency investigations or adjudications; Congress is less interested in Inspector General audits of federal contractors than in investigations of a political official; and courts seldom if ever grant private motions to quash administrative subpoenas on grounds that an agency has exceeded its statutory authority. These phenomena reflect the absence of administrative procedures governing the executive branch's investigative process.[92]

[92] Consider a contemporary anecdote reflecting administrative procedures and congressional norms reflecting bureaucratic investigations and enforcement as not subject to political control by Congress. On July 23, 2014, the Chair of the Senate Committee on Commerce sent a letter to the Chair of the House Committee on Oversight and Government Reform, declaring that the Oversight Chair engaged in "interference" in an administrative trial by the FTC and stated, "[i]t is not the job of Congress to serve as an advocate for one particular side and attempt to sway a judge[.]" Letter from Senator John Rockefeller to Representative Darrell Issa (July 23, 2014), *available at* https://oversight.house.gov/sites/democrats.oversight.house.gov/files/migrated/uploads/Chairman%20Rockefeller%20to%20Chairman%20Issa%2007-23-14.pdf. Senate Rule 43 states, "a Member of the Senate … has the right to assist petitioners before executive and independent government officials and agencies" and may "request information[,] urge prompt consideration[,] express judgments[,] and call for reconsideration of an administrative response which the Member believes is not reasonably supported by statutes, regulations or considerations of equity or public policy[.]" The U.S. House of Representatives Standard of Conduct permit members' "intervening with federal agencies and personnel" and describes the "variety of options" available to a Member who seeks to affect an ongoing legal proceeding. *See* House Committee on Ethics, Congressional Standards, *available at* https://ethics.house.gov/casework/congressional-standards. But the Administrative Procedure Act states that "no interested person outside the agency shall

The results identified in this chapter further inform how scholars think about questions of congressional control over executive branch policy by introducing new variables, e.g., grants of investigative powers, to the literature. Congress's power to investigate the private sector in order to craft public policy is at risk of abdication even if such abdication does not substantively enhance oversight efficiency. More law enforcement powers for the executive branch to use against businesses may advance electoral interests (the FDA's investigation of Juul or the EPA's investigation of BP surely led to congressional credit-claiming opportunities through oversight) but it disregards the importance of investigations for the purpose of legislative reform. Furthermore, even to the extent that the congressional choice to increase executive law enforcement discretion advances congressional oversight efficiency, there is no real sense in which Congress can investigate law enforcement—a "function committed exclusively to the president by the Constitution".[93]

The solution to this problem of abdication may lie in administrative procedures. Under the Administrative Procedure Act, 5 U.S.C. § 551(4), a "rule" includes "the whole or a part of an agency statement of general or particular applicability and future effect designed to implement, interpret, or prescribe law or policy[.]" As the Supreme Court articulated in *Oklahoma Press Publishing v. Walling*, agency investigations are aimed at determining the coverage of a statute to certain conduct in order to bring a complaint, not a final disposition. Just as *McGrain v. Daugherty* conceived of the legislative "power of inquiry" over the private sphere to be "an essential and appropriate auxiliary to the legislative function",[94] the *Oklahoma Press Publishing* Court similarly understood administrative subpoenas to be essential to prescribing policy.[95] Both decisions occurred prior to the enactment of the Administrative Procedure Act but both

make or knowingly cause to be made to any member of the body comprising the agency, administrative law judge, or other employee who is or may reasonably be expected to be involved in the decisional process of the proceeding, an *ex parte* communication relevant to the merits of the proceeding." 5 U.S.C. § 557(d)(1)(A). 5 U.S.C. § 557(d)(2) specifically states, "[t]his subsection does not constitute authority to withhold information from Congress." Notwithstanding Senate rules and the Administrative Procedure Act, congressional oversight norms do not consider bureaucratic enforcement and adjudication to be within the power of Congress to supervise.

[93] *Memorandum Opinion for the Counsel to the President*, *supra* note 85.

[94] 273 U.S. 135, 174 (1927).

[95] 327 U.S. 186 (1946).

decisions make clear that the legislative power of inquiry is bound by administrative procedures which require publication of the rule which authorizes or justifies the investigation.

The jurisprudential justification or rejection of congressional delegation depending on the legislative power in question is ripe for clarification given the passage of the Administrative Procedure Act. The Supreme Court's instruction in *J. W. Hampton, Jr., & Co. v. United States*[96] that "[i]f Congress shall lay down by legislative act an intelligible principle to which the person or body authorized to fix such rates is directed to conform, such legislative action is not a forbidden delegation of legislative power" can be addressed through administrative procedures as can the Court's statement in *Watkins v. United States* that "a [congressional] investigation into individual affairs is invalid if unrelated to any legislative purpose. That is beyond the powers conferred upon the Congress in the Constitution."[97] Once the investigative power of Congress is delegated, the intelligible principle governing its grant is the procedural requirement that jurisdiction and the obligations of regulated parties be stated publicly *as a rule of law*, in advance of investigations against citizens or corporations.

While the administrative procedures established under the Administrative Procedure Act collapse the distinction between presidential law enforcement departments and legislative agencies, for indeed both entities engage in rulemaking and are subject to the APA, the distinction may be relevant to discretionary decisions by agencies concerning requests for information which are based on standards of "particular applicability" designed to "prescribe" "policy." Otherwise, the congressional experiment in creating a regulatory state to enhance policy while developing legislative oversight to control such policy will have begun as an investigative state, matured into an administrative state, and will end as an enforcement state unmotivated to advance policy for the general welfare despite the electoral gains it promises to members.

[96] 276 U.S. 394, 409 (1928).

[97] 354 U.S. 178, 198 (1957).

Appendix A: Measuring Oversight

Current methods used by scholars assessing oversight of the bureaucracy run into practical problems with variable selection (or transformation in order to interpret parameter coefficients). For example, in using ideological divergence as a variable, scholars rely upon DW-NOMINATE scores to calculate an index of distance from the ideology of the chair or committee ideological median and the bureaucracy. But DW-NOMINATE scores are based on legislative votes; thus accounting for ideological divergence between chairs and regulators based on such scores presumes that members conducting oversight can adequately price that distance, which, in effect, says little if true: agencies do not engage in floor votes and even if the president's ideology were the proxy for the ideology of the bureaucracy, the idea that a given chair will hold a hearing based upon ideological distance means that oversight is uninfluenced by *actual* agency action, just by perceived ideology. This presents obvious external validity problems: a given order of hearings by a committee is then determined by ideological distance, not external events like agency infractions. Moreover, such models assume that positions informed by floor votes are an accurate proxy of agency decision-making. This latter assumption is belied by the modern nature of independent investigative agencies purportedly insulated from presidential control: the federal courts have held that all agencies must make decisions without evidence of "political taint" and independent agencies have specific rules governing *ex parte* communications.[98]

The risk with these models is that what gets measured is not necessarily the effect of ideological distance between the bureaucracy and Congress on oversight but the effects of chair or median committee ideology on the likelihood for oversight over the president through the agencies and departments (as-if some instrumental variable), which ultimately does little to expand current knowledge. As previously stated, if ideological distance is the key causal motivator for oversight, then the oversight

[98] The Supreme Court has held that most "independent" agencies are captured by congressional preferences. *FCC v. Fox Television Stations*, 129 S. Ct. 1800, 1815 (2009) ("independent agencies are sheltered not from politics, but from the president, and … their freedom from presidential oversight (and protection) has simply been replaced by increased subservience to congressional direction"). Methodological approaches relying on ideology that seek to account for the entire Executive branch may, by default, only measure the political departments.

agenda exists both *ex ante* and *a priori* which means that the variable identification itself assumes, without proof, the invalidity of *a posteriori* agenda-setting like fire alarms. Such a theory would have to explain why Congress, with such omniscience, does not simply execute legislative rules to sanction predictable ideological infractions before investing heavily in oversight work. In political terms, Congressional Review Act oversight over agency rules would be unnecessary because Congress could simply pass laws invalidating foreseeable statutory interpretations that go against the political preferences of the congressional majority.

Other scholars, like Brian Feinstein, look at the effects on congressional hearings of "agency infractions".[99] Identifying agency infractions primarily from government reports and media like those produced by Inspectors General, the Government Accountability Office and news editorials and measuring the effects of those infractions on the likelihood of a congressional hearing simply measures the likelihood that Congress selects hearing content, in part, from statutorily required reports.

The theory of oversight as a response to agency infractions assumes that a committee's initial decision is to hold a hearing or ignore the infraction.[100] This theoretical generalization fails to appreciate that, as a practical matter, the mere presentation to an agency head of an Inspector General's findings from audits, investigations or administrative reviews has causal effects on agency change independent from hearing activity. In fact, every Inspector General semiannual report is required to identify those IG recommendations from the current fiscal year that have been adopted by the agency as well as disclose those IG recommendations from the prior fiscal year that have not been followed by the agency. Thus, any data measuring shared topics in these semiannual reports and congressional hearings and then measuring the effectiveness of those hearings on resolving agency infractions may simply be measuring infractions that were cured independent of a hearing.

Feinstein's (2018) data generation strategy, where he "hand-coded each item" on the GAO "Top Management Challenges lists"[101] makes

[99] *See* Brian D. Feinstein, *Congress in the Administrative State*, 95 Wash. U. L. Rev. 1187 (2018) (I used the pagination at the public version, *available at* https://chicagounbound.uchicago.edu/cgi/viewcontent.cgi?article=2507&context=law_and_economics#page=24).

[100] *Id.* at 19.

[101] *Supra* note 10 at note 88.

assumptions that may obscure causal inferences. First, GAO does not produce the "Top Management Challenges" lists, the IGs, required under the Reports Consolidation Act of 2000[102] produce the "Top Management and Performance Challenges" (TMPC) reports. The TMPC reports are separate from the IG semiannual reports. Second, while all Inspectors General must submit semiannual reports to Congress, the IGs at government corporations, legislative branch agencies, and certain other federal entities are exempt from issuing TMPC reports. For agency infractions identified by independent agency IGs (those at boards like the NLRB, SEC, etc.) in their semiannual reports, there will be a gap in the data because none of those agencies produce TMPC reports. One possibility is that Feinstein collected data from the GAO "high risk" list published at the beginning of every Congress. When discussing IG semiannual reports, GAO lists, and *New York Times* and *Wall Street Journal* articles, Feinstein states (and cites Joel Aberbach's work for support), "legislator and staff surveys suggest that overseers actually rely on these four sources when setting their oversight agendas."[103] Of course, it would be impossible for Aberbach to have argued that congressional staff relied on the GAO "high risk" list because the list was not developed until after Aberbach's study was completed.[104] Second, Table 4-5 on page 88 (which page 89 references) in Aberbach's study on oversight agenda-setting does not specify either GAO or OIGs as "governmental sources."

Furthermore, there is already a statutory mechanism for bureaucratic agents invested with legislative power to report agency infractions. Under the IG Act, an IG must report "immediately" to the agency head when the IG becomes aware of "particularly serious or flagrant problems, abuses, or deficiencies relating to the administration of programs and operations."[105] In turn, the agency head must transmit that report to the committees or subcommittees of Congress with jurisdiction over the agency within seven calendar days ("seven-day letters"). Accounting for these letters would be the best evidence of "agency infractions" because they (1) are not based on recommendations found in reports that could

[102] 31 U.S.C. § 3105, *note.*

[103] *Accord.* Joel Aberbach, *Keeping a Watchful Eye: The Politics of Congressional Oversight* (1990) at 89.

[104] *See* GAO 2019 High Risk List, Appendix I "What Is the History of the High-Risk Program?" *available at* https://www.gao.gov/assets/700/697245.pdf#page=76.

[105] 5 U.S.C. Appx. § 5(d).

be corrected by the agency and (2) would be the equivalent of an exogenous shock to Congress, avoid endogeneity problems with other government reports (or causal influence by Congress itself), and could be easily tracked as to whether Congress subsequently acts. There is also the problem of timing: given Congress can, at any time, access information of agency infractions from Offices of Inspector General, why would Congress wait for a semiannual report? And even if Congress would wait for that report (itself retrospective of the prior half-fiscal year), and assuming the congressional oversight agenda was primarily informed by information in these reports, then what explains variation between the actual committee agenda at the end of a session from the required, publicly released committee agenda at the beginning of that session?

In addition to the issues identified above, there are two additional problems with relying on GAO reports: First, all GAO reports are within the discretion of the Comptroller General[106] which means they are not "politically insulated" and second, the IG Act, as amended, requires each Inspector General to "give particular regard to the activities of the Comptroller General of the United States with a view toward avoiding duplication and ensuring effective coordination and cooperation."[107] If GAO does an investigation at the request of a member, the relevant OIG will not engage which effectively means deference to a member or staff-directed inquiry. As a practical matter, it is therefore not the case that "the possibility of congressional influence in [IG subjects] are not present, since these offices are considered removed from congressional influence."[108] IGs, GAO, and regulatory enforcement agencies are exercising legislative authority and, in particular, IG and GAO investigations of the bureaucracy are part and parcel of congressional oversight.

That legislative personnel who staff hearings and investigations may rely on government reports, like GAO or Inspector General reports, in setting the initial oversight plan does not prove a causal direction: regulators will often set their own fiscal year agendas based upon the

[106] 31 U.S.C. § 717(b). The Comptroller General has interpreted this broad for evaluation authority to permit him to conduct audits and investigations at the request of any member of Congress as such would be "on the initiative of the Comptroller General".

[107] 5 U.S.C. Appendix § 4(c).

[108] Feinstein, *supra* note 10 at 1211. Note also that OIGs are required to report to Congress through over 20 separate provisions, 5 U.S.C. Appx. §§ 4(a)(2), 5(a)(1)–(22).

congressional hearings from the prior year.[109] Hearing topics might be chosen through a combination of selecting the perennial issues raised in government reports and unique characteristics of whether a given committee leader is risk-averse or risk-tolerant. In short, in examining the likelihood that an agency infraction *causes* an oversight hearing, a necessary control is the list of hearing topics by a given committee in a prior congressional session. Alternatively, conditions of divided or unified government may affect willingness, throughout a given session, to depart from a standard repertoire of waste, fraud, or abuse issues.

Additionally, issues in a given oversight plan may be repeat issues and the effect of a given variable on oversight may be related to the number of years the committee leader has served in Congress or the variable is itself a function of some product between the rate of change of its prior congressional session values with the prior values of the dependent variable. While these issues of error distribution can be assisted by interpretive techniques, certain of those interpretations may strain generalizability, replicability, and predictability. For instance, theoretical models that combine assumptions about bureaucratic control and ideological conflict may overgeneralize in ways that can have some predictability for hearings by committees with limited oversight jurisdiction, i.e., financial regulators, but poor predictability for those committees with no limitations in oversight jurisdiction, like the Senate Committee on Homeland Security and Government Affairs or the House Oversight and Reform Committee.

Given both hearing-level and Congress-level covariates, a multilevel empirical model may identify unobserved group-level effects on the dependent variable. Indeed, in the case of congressional hearings, hearings occur within a context broader than any given hearing: which Committee is holding the hearing? Is it in the House or Senate? Which political party has the majority? What's the party of the president? It is reasonable to expect that those hearings occurring during the same Congress will be more highly correlated with one another than they are with hearings in different Congresses. Given the perceived nesting of hearings as level one observations within observed Congresses at level

[109] *See e.g.*, HHS OIG, Semiannual Report to Congress—April 1, 2019 through September 30, 2019 at 13 (identifying all testimony from the OIG before Congress in the covered reporting period), ***available at*** https://oig.hhs.gov/reports-and-publications/archives/semiannual/2019/2019-fall-sar.pdf#page=16.

two, a multilevel model specification warrants some discussion. A motivation for using multilevel models is to account for observations that but for the explicit nesting of data may not have uncorrelated residuals.[110] The clustering of hearing phenomena by Congress is a natural factor of legislative terms and would not readily resolve any risks of correlation among observations across Congresses. Committee Chairmen in both chambers may serve 2, 4- or 6-year terms, meaning Committee chairs could change mid-Congress, so some hearings within a given Congress may have residuals that are more highly correlated with observations from surrounding Congresses rather than observations from other hearings even within that Committee or congressional term. Further, while Congress-level data may form one group, the topics of the hearings or the committee holding the hearing may form others, suggesting that hearings are not intrinsically nested in any one descriptive group once one determines to not defer to the formal delineations of the Legislative Reorganization Act. Criteria like year, Congress, subcommittee, topic, or subtopic reflect the multiplicity of ways in which a given hearing can be considered grouped within a secondary unit.

For the purposes of identifying models in order to make generalizable political inferences or predictions, using Congress-level and hearing-level hierarchical modeling would suggest that one is interested in restricting hearing-level coefficients' predictions on duration by Congress-level effects. But the empirical focus should be on covariate effects across Congresses and treated by an as-if random intervention. Hierarchical effects on covariates, whether Congress, Committee, subcommittee, or subtopic are not expected to reveal meaningful effects from a prediction perspective.[111]

McGrath's (2013) strategy of identifying oversight hearings by keywords rather than jurisdiction shows total oversight hearing days per year as increasing over time in contradiction to my data, *above* (Fig. 6).

In distinction to McGrath's (2013) data, my measure of the data (Fig. 7) and Kriner and Schicker's (2014) measure of the data (Fig. 8) are consistent.

[110] Finch, Holmes, Bolin, & Kelley, *Multilevel Modeling Using R* (2014).

[111] Afshartous & de Leeuw, *Prediction in Multilevel Models*, 30 J. Educ. Behav. Stat. No. 2 (2005) at 109–139.

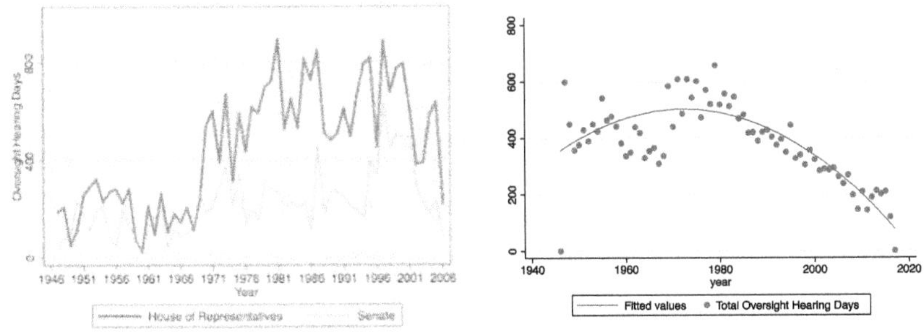

Fig. 6 Comparisons to McGrath (2013) data

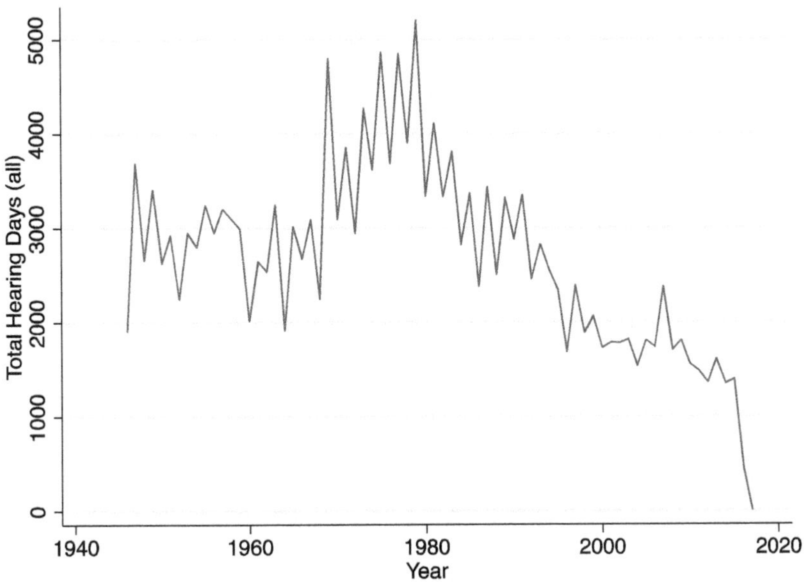

Fig. 7 Total congressional hearing days per year (All Policy Agendas Observations)

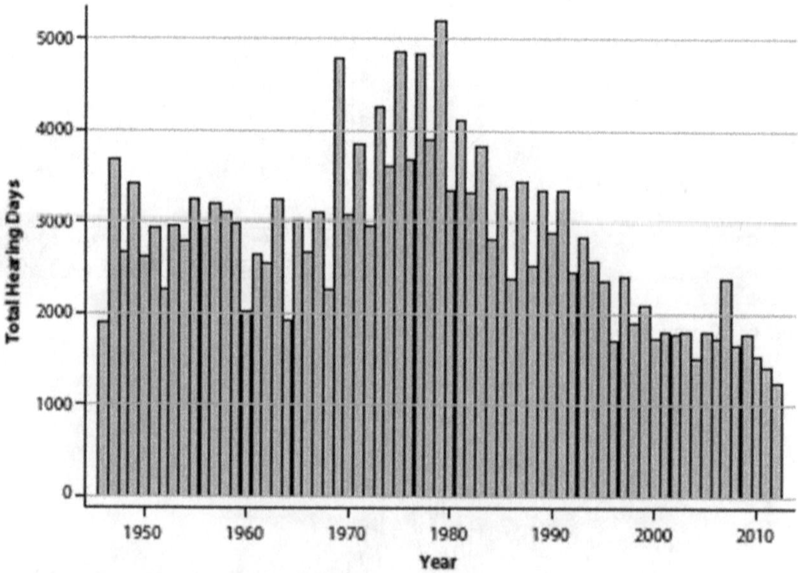

Fig. 8 Kriner and Schickler's (2014) measure of total congressional hearing days

Further, as Figs. 9 and 10 show, adding my measure for the pre-IG versus post-IG act period to the Kriner and Schickler (2014, 2016) data and interacting that variable with their divided government variable cancels out Kriner and Schickler's reported effects caused by divided government.

Adding the passage of the IG Act as a key independent variable to Kriner and Schicker's model reveals that divided government does not have independent effects on investigations of the president once the IG Act is passed. Further, as Fig. 11 shows, the Kriner and Schickler data confirms that after passage of the IG Act, the time spent by Congress on investigative hearings decreased.

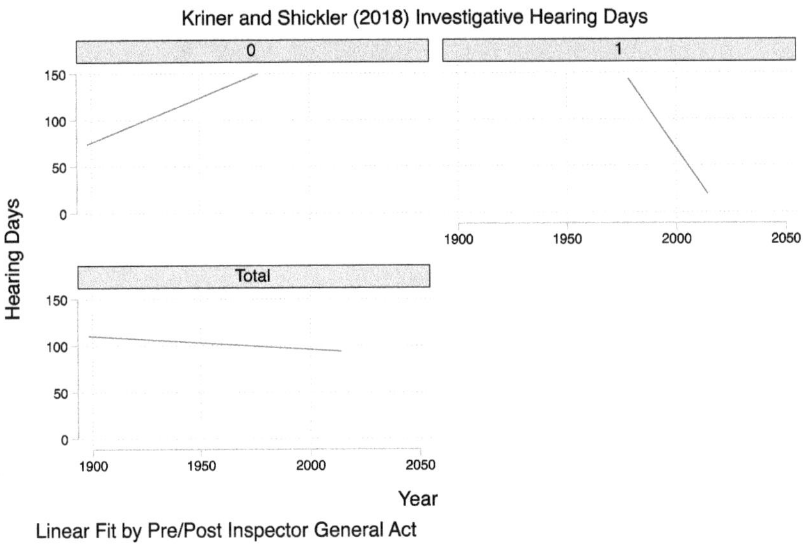

Fig. 9 Kriner and Schickler investigative hearing days before and after passage of the IG Act

Appendix B: Additional Models of Effects of Investigative Delegation on Oversight Efficiency

The administrative subpoena data is interesting in its own right. The Department of Transportation has the most administrative subpoena authority, followed by Agriculture, Health and Human Services, EPA, Commerce, Labor, Interior, and Energy, respectively. Of those agencies, the only Senate permanent subcommittee with related oversight jurisdiction is the Senate Environment and Public Works subcommittee on oversight and investigations which has jurisdiction over the EPA. As was observed from the Policy Agendas data, however, this subcommittee was coded 0 for total hearings per year from 1946–2020. In the U.S. House of Representatives, standing oversight subcommittees exist for the Department of Energy, Interior, Commerce and EPA. Again, the three largest agencies in terms of administrative subpoena authority are Transportation, Agriculture, and Health and Human Services, which have more statutory subpoena authority than all other agencies combined, yet no

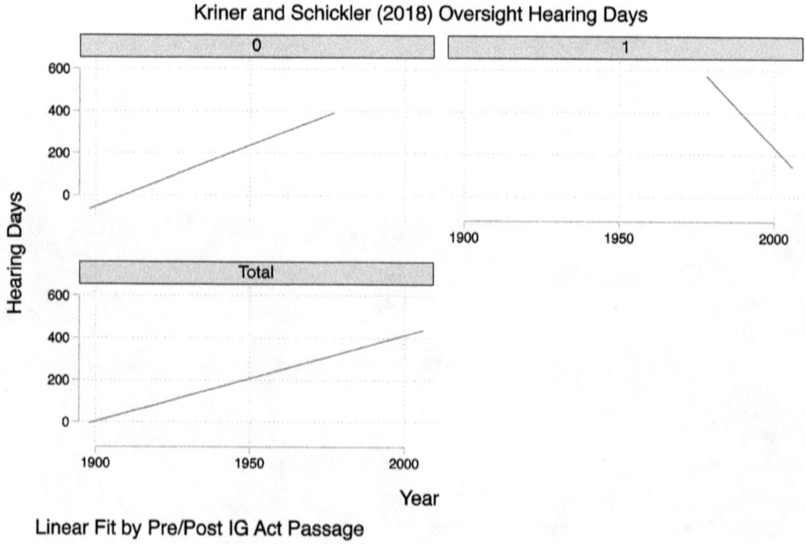

Fig. 10 Kriner and Schickler oversight hearing days before and after passage of the IG Act

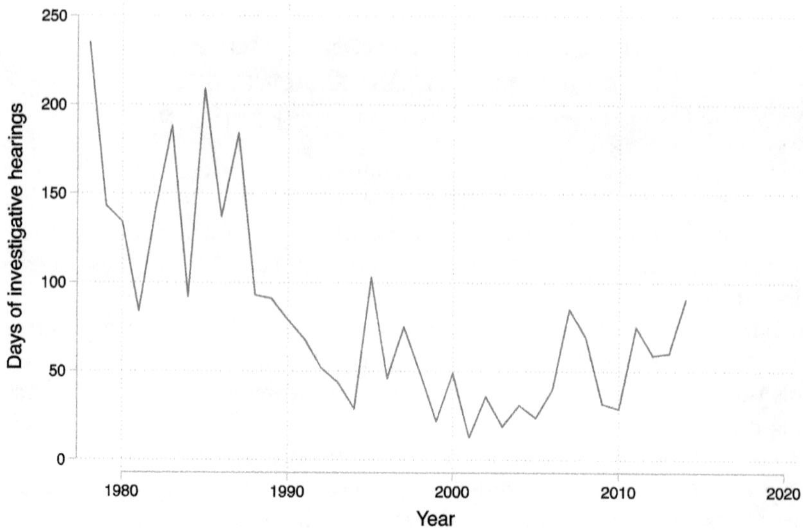

Fig. 11 Kriner and Schickler misconduct hearing days after passage of the IG Act

permanent oversight or investigations subcommittees at either the House of Representatives or the Senate exists with jurisdiction over these agencies. Interestingly, when DOJ reported its subpoena data to Congress, it relied both on agency self-reports as well as its own independent analysis. DOJ reported that the Department of Transportation (DOT) had two statutory authorities the DOT was unaware existed, Agriculture had 1, but EPA had 4, Commerce 6, Labor 3, and Interior 5. This suggests, at least anecdotally, that these agencies have more subpoena power than they realize and therefore utilize. This motivates the significance of administrative subpoenas as a variable: they are delegated authorities from Congress which the agencies use for investigating regulatory infractions, but the structure of oversight jurisdiction has been designed to limit substantive review of these powers.

To further test my finding of no effects of investigative delegations by Congress on oversight efficiency, I run additional models without instrumenting subpoenas through rules and without a leading dependent variable as well as examine the number of hearings in addition to days, which are reflected in Table 4.

Table 4 shows the results of five alternative models of the examined independent variables to check the inferences made from Table 1. In these models, annual administrative subpoena authorizations are not considered to affect oversight hearing length as instrumented through rulemaking. Further, in four of the models, the hearing length dependent variable is not converted into a leading variable (where the independent variables in a given year would be predicting subsequent year hearing lengths). As such, the models conceive of subpoena authorizations as a congressional choice to increase oversight efficiency independent of the effects of bureaucratic policymaking and thus concurrent with expected changes in hearing activity. In the first model, the total number of oversight hearing days per year decreases when post-Inspector General Act oversight hearings increase in likelihood (statistically significant at a 0.001 level) yet increases as rulemaking (0.01 level) and subpoena authorizations (0.05 level) increase. This would tend to confirm the Table 1 results supporting Hypothesis 2 but lead us to confirm the rejection of Hypothesis 1, for we observe investigative delegations by Congress decreasing oversight efficiency by forcing each oversight hearing to take more time.

The second model replicates the first but includes the indicator variables for which party controls the House, Senate and presidency. Like the first model, we observe statistically significant effects in decreases in

Table 4 Delegation on number of and length of oversight hearings (incl. non-leading DV) (1946–2020)

	(1)	(2)	(3)	(4)	(5)
	Total oversight hearing days (per year)	*Total oversight hearing days (per year)*	*Total oversight hearings (per year)*	*Total oversight hearings (per year)*	*Total oversight hearings per year (leading indicator)*
Pre v. Post IG Act	−0.554***	−0.454***	0.448***	0.416***	0.437***
	(0.116)	(0.113)	(0.0864)	(0.0868)	(0.0740)
Total agency rules	0.0000**	0.0000	0.0000**	0.0000*	0.0000*
	(0.0000)	(0.0000)	(0.0000)	(0.0000)	(0.0000)
Administrative subpoena-authorizing statutes	0.00847*	0.00795*	0.00490	0.00829*	0.00473**
	(0.00396)	(0.00363)	(0.00330)	(0.00350)	(0.00167)
House Party identification		0.312***		−0.128	
		(0.0877)		(0.0744)	
Senate Party identification		−0.254**		−0.0476	
		(0.0776)		(0.0648)	
Party identification of the president		−0.0955		−0.190**	
		(0.0940)		(0.0724)	
Constant	5.864***	5.904***	4.360***	4.594***	4.452***
	(0.0704)	(0.155)	(0.0690)	(0.120)	(0.0538)
/					
lnalpha	−1.338*	−1.442*	−2.413***	−2.550***	−3.192***
	(0.605)	(0.685)	(0.597)	(0.614)	(0.188)
Observations	72	72	72	72	70
Adjusted R^2					

Standard errors in parentheses
$^{*}p < 0.05$, $^{**}p < 0.01$, $^{***}p < 0.001$

annual oversight days as post-Inspector General Act oversight hearings increase in likelihood but increases in annual oversight days as subpoena authorizations increase. We do not observe a statistically significant effect on oversight days from bureaucratic rulemaking. But we do observe a Democratic party-controlled House as increasing hearing days with a Democratic party-controlled Senate as decreasing them at statistically significant levels. Because, as a general rule, Democratic party control of the Senate means the Democrats have control of either the White House or the House, the decreased likelihood of pure divided government in those circumstances helps explain reductions of the duration of oversight hearings. This effect would be distinct from the one where the House is Democratically controlled and divided government exists, for such conditions might lead to less efficient but more in-depth oversight. Of course, if the preference is to maximize the incidence of annual oversight hearings by reducing the time spent per hearing, then it would appear that conditions of divided government prevent such preference maximization.

The next two models in Table 4 consider the number or incidence of congressional oversight hearings per year as the dependent variable rather than the length of hearings. Here, we observe the reverse concerning the Inspector General Act passage indicator, where, as the likelihood of post-Inspector General Act hearings increases, the likelihood of holding more oversight hearings increases (supporting the preference maximization theory of oversight efficiency). In this model, administrative subpoena authorizations have no effect on the number of hearings but rulemaking increases the number of hearings at a statistically significant level. This evidence provides further reasons to disconfirm Hypothesis 1 and conclude that investigative delegations either do not affect or decrease oversight efficiency (legislative preference for more hearings). Interestingly, when we replicate this model and add in the party identification factors, we see that subpoena delegations, as well as rulemaking and Inspector General Act enactment, increase oversight efficiency at statistically significant levels. This same phenomenon is observed in the final (fifth) model where the total oversight hearings per year is converted into a leading variable and where the party identification factors are dropped from the model.

The disjunction between subpoena delegations and the effects of the Inspector General Act appears puzzling given that both variables would be proxies for the effects of bureaucratic investigations on oversight efficiency. Yet Fig. 4 makes clear that annual subpoena authorizations have remained fairly constant over the last 70 years. Yet consistent year-to-year unique subpoena-authorization enactments permit increasing annual subpoena activity by the bureaucracy as a single authority can permit limitless investigations, which explains how an active Inspector General community can increase Congress's electoral interests.

Given the models above restrict oversight hearings based on jurisdictional definitions, the fact that subpoena delegations may increase oversight committee and subcommittee workload may be suggestive of the role of party leadership in using non-jurisdictional committees for oversight to secure more numerous, less evidence- and document-intensive, and more election- and media-oriented hearings. On this point, I repeat the model but substitute an oversight hearing (length and incidence) proxy mirroring the ones developed by Smith (2003) and Feinstein (2009), which looks at keywords and topics to model oversight.[112] I present the results of such a model in Table 5.

What the first model in Table 5 shows is that as the definition of oversight hearing expands to cover hearings beyond those committees and subcommittees whose oversight jurisdiction is authorized by cameral rules, but which instead defines oversight in terms of the content of the hearing, investigative delegations by Congress increase the total number of such hearings at a statistically significant level. In other words, the pattern of administrative subpoena grants, which leads to continuous investigative activities by quasi-legislative enforcement agencies and Offices of Inspectors General, relates negatively to a pattern of hearings constrained by jurisdiction (Table 1 models) and positively toward a pattern of hearing unconstrained by jurisdiction but classified on the basis of content. The problem with such a model for oversight is that consistent with the work of Feinstein (2013), leadership appoints members to oversight committees and subcommittees. That means that hearings occurring outside of these committees are not led by members who seek a perch on an oversight-empowered committee and with staff experienced in conducting investigations of the bureaucracy. What models relying upon hearing content-based proxies for oversight are tracking, as does the one at Table 5, is not the effect of delegation on total oversight hearings but the effects of delegation on hearings which may relate to executive branch infractions unrelated to administrative subpoenas and which may exclude committee investigations (part of oversight) into statutory violations by businesses. Consider that the Inspector General Act indicator has no effect on a content-based hearing model seeking to predict effect on the total number of oversight hearings per year (Table 5, model 2). Because Feinstein argues oversight hearings take more time and may

[112] Smith, *supra* note 59; Feinstein, *supra* note 6.

Table 5 Effects of investigative delegation on oversight hearing incidence and length (content-based measure of oversight)

	(1)	(2)	(3)
	Total oversight hearings (by content analysis)	*Total oversight hearings (by content analysis)*	*Total oversight duration (by content analysis)*
Total agency rules	0.0000***	0.0000**	0.0000***
	(0.0000)	(0.0000)	(0.0000)
Administrative subpoena-authorizing statutes	0.00472***	0.00504***	0.0105*
	(0.00131)	(0.00148)	(0.00418)
Oversight hearing indicator (by topic)	0.0749***	0.0735***	0.0238
	(0.0162)	(0.0163)	(0.0189)
Gridlock		−0.000541	0.00602**
		(0.00142)	(0.00194)
Oversight duration (by topic)	−0.00384	−0.00296	0.0169**
	(0.00437)	(0.00348)	(0.00514)
Pre v. Post IG Act		0.0130	−0.672***
		(0.0928)	(0.112)
Constant	4.031***	4.051***	4.618***
	(0.0740)	(0.102)	(0.127)
/			
lnalpha	−2.746***	−2.749***	−2.153***
	(0.248)	(0.250)	(0.189)
Observations	100,206	100,206	100,206

Standard errors in parentheses
$^{*}p < 0.05$, $^{**}p < 0.01$, $^{***}p < 0.001$

promise less electoral rewards than other types of hearings, that subpoena delegations increase the numerosity of agency infraction hearings by committees without oversight jurisdiction nevertheless would be consistent with a finding that hearings within committees with jurisdictional oversight decrease as investigative delegations increase.

But this discrepancy is why looking at duration, over numerosity, is crucial in examining covariate effects on oversight. Once we replace the oversight proxy with a duration variable rather than a numerosity variable, we see that subpoena delegations increase the amount of time spent per Congress on oversight hearings within jurisdictional committees even when total oversight hearings held by those committees decreases (Table 4, models 1 and 2).

Model 3 in Table 5 develops the dependent variable via a method for measuring oversight duration replicating the approach used by McGrath (2013). With both hearing occurrence and hearing length dependent variables, we see that investigative delegations by Congress increases the amount of time Congress must spend on oversight hearings.[113] In Table 4, we see that statutory enactment of the Inspector General Act decreases the duration of jurisdictional oversight hearings, while increasing the incidence of oversight hearings per year. Once we use a formal definition of oversight, administrative subpoena statutory passage increases oversight hearing duration at a statistically significant level. Regulatory delegations in the form of agency rulemaking have parallel effects on both oversight hearing duration and numerosity.

Appendix C: Checking Robustness of DDD Model via Placebos

To test whether alternative years (placebo effects) have causal effects on oversight efficiency, I use both 1970 and 1988 as test years. The 1970 "placebo" clearly violates the parallel trends assumption as there are inconsistent changes in variation between oversight and non-oversight hearing days prior to the 1970 "Inspector General Act." With the 1988 placebo, the fact that the treatment appears to begin before 1988 (for, otherwise, hearing days dropped by over 500 in a single year) violates the assumption that treatment effects are exogenous to the data (Figs. 12 and 13).

I also test the substantive effects of the placebos and in both cases find less substantive effects on oversight efficiency from the placebo effects than from the actual treatment effect of the 1978 Act. Further, the fact that the 1988 amendments to the IG Act, which added IGs at independent agencies, did not increase the difference in differences between oversight and non-oversight hearing duration at the level of the 1978 Act is indicative of the unique differences in information provided to congressional oversight committees by, e.g., the State Department IG versus the

[113] Note that McGrath (2013), *infra*, measures total oversight hearing days using a similar approach for identifying oversight hearings as Smith (2003).

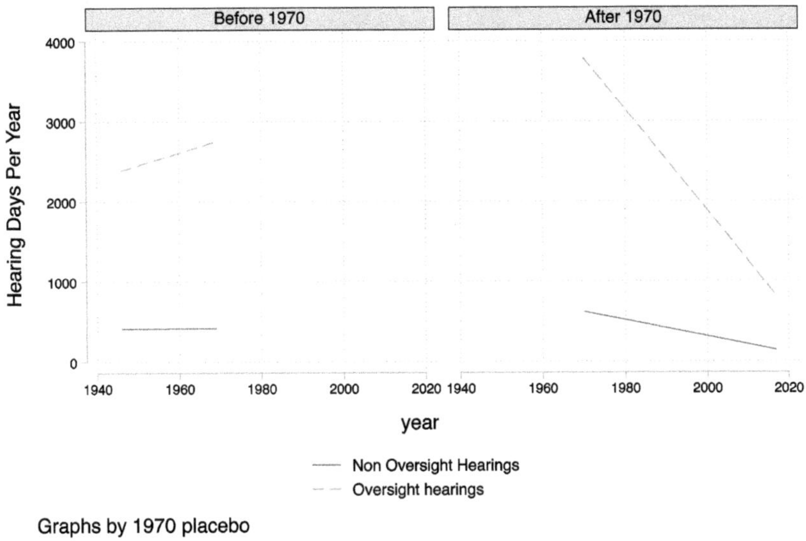

Fig. 12 Effects on oversight if treatment was in 1970

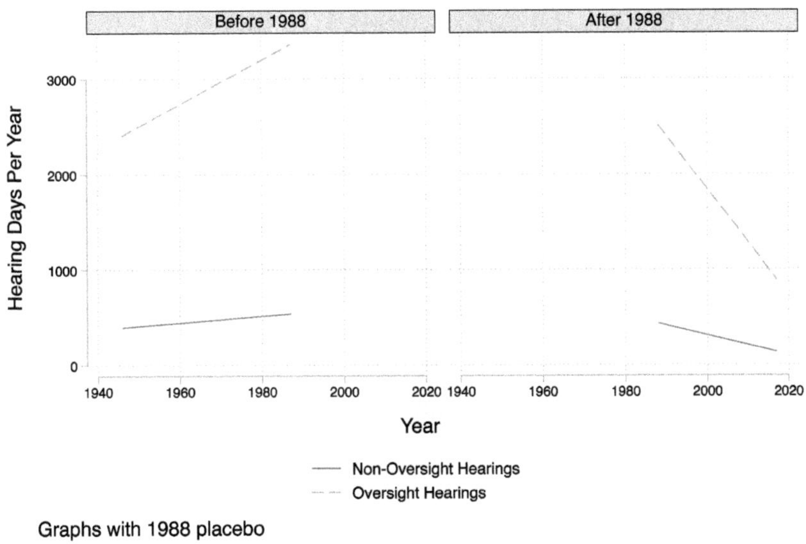

Fig. 13 Effects on oversight if treatment was in 1988

Table 6 Placebo effects on differences between oversight and non-oversight hearing efficiency

	(1) 1970 Placebo	*(2) 1988 Placebo*
	Hearing length (in days)	*Hearing length (in days)*
Difference-in-differences estimate of the treatment effect	−1.908***	−1.291***
	(0.0602)	(0.048)
Pre-treatment non-oversight hearings	2.464***	2.284***
	(0.01)	(0.01)
Observations	98,950	98,950
Adjusted R^2	0.064	0.09

Standard errors in parentheses
$^{*}p < 0.05$, $^{**}p < 0.01$, $^{***}p < 0.001$

NLRB IG: the former allows for legislative attacks on a cabinet officer while the latter does not (Table 6).

Appendix D: Additional Checks on Law Enforcement Effects on Oversight Efficiency

See Table 7.

Table 7 Effects of law enforcement on per-hearing oversight efficiency

	(1) Negative binomial regression	*(2) Negative binomial regress (leading DV)*	*(3) Instrumental variable design (subpoenas instrumented through enforcement cases)*	*(4) Instrumental variable model (subpoenas affecting oversight through enforcement)* ***(Weighted by SD)***
	Duration per oversight hearing	*Total oversight hearing days per congress (leading indicator)*	*Duration per oversight hearing*	*Future oversight hearing days*
Federal criminal cases filed (per year)	−0.0000***	−0.0000***	−0.0000**	−0.362***
	(0.0000)	(0.0000)	(0.0000)	(0.0328)
Constant	1.929***	1.928***	1.840***	0.726***
	(0.0787)	(0.0791)	(0.238)	(0.0694)
/				
lnalpha	−0.969***	−0.969***		−15.39***
	(0.0750)	(0.0756)		(1.157)
Observations	9321	9321	9321	9321
Adjusted R^2				

Standard errors in parentheses
$^{*}p < 0.05$, $^{**}p < 0.01$, $^{***}p < 0.001$

CHAPTER 5

Punctuated Delegation and the Politics of Administrative Law

It is an accepted belief within American public law theory that the federal administrative state was developed by political progressives.[1] This belief has shaped political debates beyond the boundaries of academic theory. It is a belief that frames position-taking by legislators on questions of regulation and democratic representation and informs judicial doctrines concerning the delegation of legislative power and the constitutional separation of powers writ large.[2] This book is a descriptive investigation of the effects of delegation on the institution of congressional oversight. It is the first scholarly attempt to examine a form of delegation by Congress outside the traditionally studied model of legislative delegation of rulemaking to the executive branch. Crucially, this book departs from the conventional wisdom that the federal administrative state—conceived of as an expert nonpartisan, unelected bureaucracy establishing regulations over the private sphere—began in the early twentieth century with the New Deal.[3] Under that logic, the establishment of the Interstate Commerce Commission (ICC) in 1887 is not formative to the

[1] Blake Emerson, *The Public's Law: Origins and Architecture of Progressive Democracy* (2019).

[2] Keith E. Whittington & Jason Iuliano, *The Myth of the Nondelegation Doctrine*, 165 U. Pa. L. Rev. 379, 381–423 (2017).

[3] *See id.*

D. Z. Epstein, *The Investigative State: Regulatory Oversight in the United States*, https://doi.org/10.1007/978-3-031-38461-5_5

development of the federal administrative state. The ICC did not originate during the Progressive Era nor did it initially have rulemaking authority, instead possessing only investigative[4] and adjudicative power.[5] Additionally, the establishment and reform of the ICC was not necessarily to advance progressive principles, viz., to constrain private industry in support of consumer protection.[6] Public welfare justifications for regulation of business were, at this time, justified under the theory that certain industries, like railway transportation, were public service corporations and that the regulation of these corporations, themselves deriving their legal status from the state, was limited to the purview of the states.[7] In fact, national railroad companies pushed for the ICC to avoid the costs of the many, often inconsistent, rules promulgated by state administrative commissions.[8]

The significance of the investigative state has pedagogic implications for the academic study of congressional oversight. Political scientists and even federal courts do not often evaluate congressional oversight in terms of its historical development or relationship to the political development of the modern administrative state. But as this book has shown, that history is central to explaining contemporary issues and tensions in the law and politics of the administrative state. By examining the historical development of oversight, a more complete picture of our political institutions becomes clear. That history reflects that before Congress ever delegated its policy-writing powers to the bureaucracy, it delegated its investigative powers over the private sphere. In concluding this book,

[4] An Act to Regulate Commerce, 24 Stat. 379 (1887), §§ 12, 13, 19 and 20.

[5] *Id.*; §§ 13, 14, 15, and 17; Cincinnati Freight Bureau v. C., N. O. & T.P. Ry. Co., 7 I.C.C. Rep. 191 (1894).

[6] *See* Isaiah Leo Sharfman, *Railway Regulation: An Analysis of the Underlying Problems in Railways Economics from the Standpoint of Government Regulations* (1915) at 122 ("[t]he effective prevention of discrimination between commodities, then, depends upon the existence of a comprehensive system of regulation, with adequate ratemaking powers in the regulating body").

[7] *Id.* at 95–110, 142. *See also* William J. Novak, *New Democracy: The Creation of the Modern American State* (2022).

[8] *Id.* at 123. *Accord. Testimony of E.F. Kelley, Secretary of the Transportation Committee of the Saint Louis Merchants' Exchange, Report of the Senate Select Committee on Interstate Commerce*, 49th Cong., First Sess. (Jan. 18, 1886) at 873–877; William C. Coleman, *The Evolution of Federal Regulation of Intrastate Rates: The Shreveport Rate Cases*, 28 Harv. L. Rev. (1914) at 36–38; *Minn. Rate Cases*, 230 U.S. 352, 433 (1913).

I want to highlight how the revised picture that emerges from this project informs contemporary issues within the study of administrative and constitutional law.

1 Rethinking Congressional Oversight

"Oversight" as the term is used arises from the political need to monitor delegated power. Throughout the nineteenth century, as Congress delegated investigative powers to committees and then eventually to agencies, Congress exercised oversight by retaining the power to make rules of law even as agencies conducted investigations of the private sector. In short, legislative rulemaking was how Congress exercised oversight over the delegation of the legislative power of inquiry to an agency. When, in the early twentieth century, Congress delegated rulemaking authority to the bureaucracy, oversight subsequently became more formal—typified by the Legislative Reorganization Act, which empowered standing committees to exercise bureaucratic oversight, and the Administrative Procedure Act, which codified a series of norms governing agency law creation. As these statutes were being debated in Congress, the Supreme Court, in *Oklahoma Press Publishing v. Walling*, affirmed the historical picture of an administrative state formed through delegation and oversight in holding that agency investigations of the private sector, backed by subpoenas, were a "delegated power" by Congress "incidental to both [Congress's] general legislative and its investigative powers."[9] Thus, precisely four months before the APA became law, the Supreme Court held that administrative investigations were governed by the same requirements that applied to congressional investigations of the private sphere: where the power to compel documents and testimony is "an appropriate adjunct to the power of legislation" when cabined by a "legislative purpose" articulated in the authorizing resolution.[10] In the context of the Administrative Procedure Act, then, it should be a rather obvious principle that agency investigations must be cabined in advance by publicly noticed rules.

This book enhances our political understanding of congressional oversight in three key ways. First, congressional oversight is broadly exercised:

[9] 327 U.S. 186, 195, 214.

[10] *McGrain v. Daugherty*, 273 U.S. 161 (1927).

Congress investigates the president and his copartisan leadership (electoral oversight), it investigates the regulated public (legal oversight), and it investigates executive branch administration of laws, operations and programs (regulatory oversight). Second, while scholars recognize that Congress delegates its oversight powers to standing committees and Congress delegates its law-writing authority to federal agencies, this book shows that Congress also delegates its oversight powers to the executive branch, among others. In particular, Congress delegates its investigative powers to the bureaucracy and such delegation enhances congressional oversight efficiency. And in choosing to delegate through agency-agnostic procedures versus agency-specific ones, Congress relies on administrative procedures in delegating its oversight powers to bureaucratic watchdogs. What scholars describe as "law enforcement" activities of Inspectors General or regulatory commission are instead delegated oversight. Third, and related, the phenomenon of delegated oversight tells us something about how the congressional oversight agenda is set.

Because committees exercise their direct oversight, i.e., over the presidential administration, in an electorally interested manner, special interests and agencies with delegated oversight powers can influence Congress's oversight agenda. In order to affect that agenda, stakeholders must report information to Congress and its committees that comports with or otherwise enhances the electoral incentives of committees and their members and is likely to generate publicity for the Chairman or Ranking Member of the committee. *Ceteris paribus*, we should expect that the congressional oversight agenda, carried out by a politically responsive Chairman or Ranking Member, is focused on exposing the president and his copartisans in the administration. But because Congress delegates investigative powers to agency and public interest stakeholders, the selection of policy and bureaucratic oversight issues for which committees dedicate time, attention and resources is contingent upon the information brought to light by stakeholders. Fire-alarm oversight thus implies a pluralism. Consider that legal norms today interpret administrative subpoena language as a law enforcement power when, in 1946, it was considered part of rulemaking. The law of administrative subpoenas is conditional on whether regulated parties choose to quash administrative subpoenas on Administrative Procedure Act grounds and succeed in that endeavor. In this sense, we observe a pluralistic theory of power at play in informing the oversight agenda.

This implication for oversight agenda-setting helpfully responds to concerns that Congress, through delegation, has abdicated its legislative responsibility. If agenda-setting is a key legislative power and Congress retains that power when it comes to delegations of investigative or regulatory discretion, then Congress has not abdicated its legislative responsibility and, in fact, maybe strategically and efficiently pursuing its most highly leveraged function. Furthermore, Congress prefers to delegate the ministerial oversight function not just to its committees but to regulatory enforcement agencies and permanent government watchdogs as well as through private rights to individuals while reserving politically salient oversight to its more direct impeachment-related powers is a key implication of this book that helps explain disagreements among scholars as to whether oversight is electorally motivated or about institutional power or whether Congress continually polices for agency misconduct or is less direct in how it uses its investigative resources.

2 Rethinking the Law of Congressional Oversight

Contrary to the legal understanding of oversight as tailored to the development of legislation, oversight is not about lawmaking even if Congress's sparse regulatory investigations are. And delegation of investigative authority to bureaucratic watchdogs causally enhances the political dimensions of oversight. Because congressional oversight is a political activity distinct from regulatory investigations by Congress (those aimed at informing legislation), conflicts between Congress and the executive branch should not be judicially reviewable while conflicts between Congress and individuals by their nature present justiciable questions, albeit ones limited to stated legislative goals.[11] And because Congress delegates its investigative and oversight authority, presumptions about judicial review should extend to those powers, as delegated. That Inspector General investigations of waste, fraud, and abuse of executive branch programs are not legally enforceable, while Inspector General

[11] Daniel Z. Epstein, *Congressional Oversight Disputes as Political Questions, Part I: The Decline of the Interbranch Accommodation Doctrine*, 38 Yale J. Reg. Notice and Comment (2020), *available at* https://www.yalejreg.com/nc/congressionaloversight-disputes-as-political-questions-parti-the-decline-of-the-interbranchaccommodation-doctrine-by-daniel-epstein.

investigations of private sector contractors are, reflects Congress's own recognition of the politicized nature of oversight.

Judicial resolution of such disputes between Congress and the executive branch is attractive because, unlike political remedies, legal remedies lead to finality. The allure of resolving oversight disputes outside the political process is why clarity in the typologies of oversight is important. Scholars might agree that a congressional investigation into a pharmaceutical company's compliance with labeling requirements under the Food, Drug and Cosmetic Act or an investigation into whether an agency is complying with the Freedom of Information Act is different in kind from a congressional investigation of the bank where the president holds accounts or whether the president's call to a foreign leader constituted a "high crime or misdemeanor." But Congress considers all of these activities within the oversight typology. Even if scholars might suggest that all of these activities could be explained by electoral motivations or through Congress's interest in controlling the bureaucracy, an underspecified oversight typology presents practical problems for those who think of the president as separate from the bureaucracy or who are skeptical that Congress would invest equal resources into those inquiries likely to have electoral consequences and those that would not.

Congressional oversight targets more than just bureaucratic implementation of legislative goals: it is used to examine the political leadership of an administration as well as investigate private entities. Further, Congress delegates these oversight powers strategically to enable its members to maximize the electoral benefits associated with public hearings. Because Congress's public oversight activities are electorally motivated, the judge-made rules regulating how Congress and the executive branch conduct or respond to oversight may be misplaced if for no other reason than the federal courts have deemed purely political disputes between the branches to be the sorts of political questions the courts are not equipped to adjudicate.[12] The diverse options in the choice of oversight—over the private sphere, the political authority of an administration, or the bureaucracy—are oversimplified if not ignored by the judge-made requirement that congressional investigations must be cabined by a "legislative purpose." The purpose of oversight is political as are its remedies.

[12] *Nixon v. United States*, 506 U.S. 224, 226 (1993) (holding that impeachment proceedings lack judicially manageable standards).

3 The Enforcement State

The theoretical and empirical chapters of this book demonstrate how the administrative state developed through punctuations in delegation to committees, via ministerial duties to officers, and then in investigative delegations to the bureaucracy culminating in the Interstate Commerce Commission. As Fig. 1 in Chapter 2 serves to illustrate, upon the emergence of the administrative state, federal administrative law responds to three waves of institutional change: first, the Interstate Commerce Act of 1887; second, the Administrative Procedure and Legislative Reorganization Acts of 1946; and third, the post-Nixon civil service reforms of 1978. In the first wave, the administrative state is an investigative and adjudicative state lacking legislative rulemaking power over the private sphere, which is still retained by Congress. In the second wave, the administrative state is a fully legislative state subject to congressional oversight. And in the third wave, the administrative state is subsumed into the presidency, representing a unitary law enforcement state where legislative power has been fully vested in special interests.

Congressional assignment of regulatory responsibilities to executive officers is not thought to be an impermissible vesting of legislative power because executive officers lack discretion to write policy and only carry out these responsibilities through their power to enforce the law.[13] As the regulatory bureaucracy emerged, the law distinguished commissions from law enforcement departments, with the former constituting agencies of Congress.[14] When legislative policymaking by the executive branch became more ubiquitous, the law developed a distinction between the enforcement of policy[15] versus traditional notions of law enforcement involving investigations by federal officers, prosecution or complaint by the United States, and adjudication by the federal courts.[16] Prior to the enactment of the Administrative Procedure Act there appeared to be an

[13] *Marshall Field & Co. v. Clark*, 143 U.S. 649, 693 (1892).

[14] *ICC v. Brimson*, 154 U.S. 447, 474–477 (1894).

[15] *J. W. Hampton, Jr., & Co. v. United States*, 276 U.S. 394, 409 (1928).

[16] *Marshall Field & Co. v. Clark*, 143 U.S. 649, 693 (1892).

uncomplicated distinction between the bureaucracy insulated from presidential control[17] and the law enforcement departments subject to the president's supervision.[18]

Unitary executive theorists bristle at such circumstances because they believe when Congress empowers the president to appoint and remove an agency head, that agency is subject to presidential control. To say an agency run by a presidentially appointed officer is insulated from presidential control dilutes executive power. Informed by this theory of executive sovereignty, the third wave of American administrative law emerges after the Nixon presidency, culminating in reforms enacted in 1978—the Ethics in Government Act, the Office of Special Counsel and Merit Systems Protection statutes, the Independent Counsel Act, the Inspector General Act, and the Presidential Records Act—which all served to depoliticize the executive branch yet at the same time made the executive branch more unitary by treating departments, establishments and commissions as "agencies."[19]

While some scholars are critical of the administrative state from the perspective that it permits Congress to unconstitutionally vest the legislative power in another branch, it is the reality that with delegation comes oversight and control of the executive branch that reveals commitment to unitary executive theory, not nondelegation concerns, as the real interest driving critics of delegation. Beyond these abstract concerns lie more concrete fears of threats to liberty interests. If legislative powers when exercised by the executive branch are considered part and parcel of law enforcement, then the executive branch's power increases at the expense of constitutional constraints that have traditionally applied to law enforcement agents. Recent litigation reflects the presidential power as increasingly zealous of exercising control over agencies engaged in

[17] *Humphrey's Ex'r v. U.S.*, 295 U.S. 602, 628 (1935).

[18] *Myers v. United States*, 272 U.S. 52, 135 (1926).

[19] The 1978 reforms can be contrasted with the Supreme Court's decision, two years earlier, in *Buckley v. Valeo*, 424 U.S. 1, 137–138 (1976), where it held, "[i]nsofar as the powers confided in the Commission are essentially of an investigative and informative nature, falling in the same general category as those powers which Congress might delegate to one of its own committees, there can be no question that the Commission as presently constituted may exercise them."

legislative functions yet willing to entertain the cost of congressional oversight if it means being able to enforce the law outside the purview of constitutional procedures.[20]

Despite the inevitable nature of this third wave of the administrative state as a unitary enforcement state, this book suggests a formal distinction between a legislative bureaucracy and the executive departments remains feasible and would preserve both legislative prerogative over policy and executive prerogative over law enforcement. But in concluding this project, I contend that the legal nature of the administrative state is determined by the organized interests and regulatory constituents who benefit from administrative procedures and fire alarms as well as those who set the congressional oversight agenda.[21] In this sense, the punctuated nature of the administrative state and subsequent expansions in administrative law have reflected greater consilience toward a pluralistic theory of regulatory power. In what remains of this conclusion, I briefly sketch the implications of administrative pluralism.

If agency investigations of businesses or political officials is a "legislative" power then such inquiries, independent of their taking place within the executive branch, can be argued to be exempt from presidential supervision and control.[22] But it is also the case that such inquiries do not constitute law enforcement activities where agencies are entitled to unreviewable discretion. Subpoena requests by agencies engaged in ministerial functions would be limited to judicial enforcement the same way congressional subpoenas of the private sphere are limited—as being bound by procedural requirements. While the federal courts have traditionally limited congressional enforcement of its investigations of the

[20] *E.g., Severino v. Biden* et al., Case 1:21-cv-00314 (D.D.C. 2021); *Trump v. Mazars USA, LLP*, 140 S. Ct. 2019, 2048 (2020); Petition for Certiorari, *Trump v. Thompson*, et al. No. 21–932 (2022).

[21] Matthew McCubbins & Thomas Schwartz, *Congressional Oversight Overlooked: Police Patrols Versus Fire Alarms*, 28 Am. J. Pol. Sci. at 166 (1984) (describing "a system of rules, procedures and informal practices that enable individual citizens and organized interest groups to examine administrative decisions.... to charge executive agencies with violating congressional goals, and to seek remedies from agencies, courts or Congress itself").

[22] *Seila Law LLC v. Consumer Financial Protection Bureau*, 140 S. Ct. 2183, 2199–2200 (2020) (acknowledging that the president has no constitutional prerogative to remove members of "multimember expert agencies that do not wield substantial executive power").

private sphere and elected officials via the necessary and proper clause and the impeachment clause, respectively, the courts have not affirmed a general power of Congress to seek judicial enforcement of investigative requests of the bureaucracy.

Agency investigations of the private sector or political officials which derive from the bureaucracy's policymaking authority can be distinguished from executive branch activities to enforce, through the courts, policies determined through rulemaking or adjudication or which fall within the law enforcement discretion of the president.[23] By viewing bureaucratic investigations and adjudications as legislative or regulatory in nature, we have observed how the existence of agency-wide, policy-agnostic administrative procedures, rather than "intelligible principles" attached to particular policymaking authorizations by Congress, can, in theory, prevent the unlawful vesting of the legislative power outside of Congress. Administrative procedures, rather than the attempt to articulate policy intent (the "intelligible principles" doctrine), permit congressional control over agents exercising legislative power without Congress granting to the agency the power to legislate, i.e., to determine public policy standards, goals or principles on its own.

While I defend a formalism in federal administrative law that demarcates the policymaking bureaucracy as legislative and thus separate and distinct from the scope of executive power, an implication of this position is that administrative procedures should not govern the president nor executive officers as they are not agents of Congress.[24] Instead, administrative procedures like the Administrative Procedure Act's rulemaking and adjudication requirements should govern only the process of making rules or orders which should be restricted to non-enforcement (in the Article II sense) agencies and their officers.[25] Once those rules or orders

[23] Kate Andrias, *The President's Enforcement Power*, 88 N.Y.U. L. Rev. 1031, 1050 (2013) ("the notion that enforcement of law is quintessentially a responsibility of the Executive Branch, and ultimately of the President, is longstanding and beyond dispute").

[24] *Kendall v. United States*, 37 U.S. 524, 610 (1838) ("[t]he executive power is vested in a President; and as far as his powers are derived from the constitution, he is beyond the reach of any other department, except in the mode prescribed by the constitution through the impeaching power").

[25] Note this was the pre-twentieth century understanding of delegation of adjudicative and investigative functions to executive officers. Jerry L. Mashaw, *Recovering American Administrative Law: Federalist Foundations, 1787–1801*, 115 Yale L.J. 1256, 1290 (2006).

are final, enforcing them should be at the sole discretion of executive officers accountable to the president. If the investigative activities of boards, commissions, Inspectors General, or the GAO are delegations of legislative power, then they are not properly classified, as a legal matter, as law enforcement activities within the executive power or under the president's constitutional supervision.[26] Enforcement of investigations which are the whole or part of an agency rule or order is a legislative question; once a rule or order, inclusive of complaints and proposed conclusions of law, is final, then its enforcement is an executive question. That the advocates of a unitary executive do not make the formal argument—that law enforcement agencies, like the president, should be categorically exempt from administrative procedures if they do not engage in legislative functions—but instead readily concede the legitimacy of both oversight and administrative law as applied to the entire executive branch reflects the extent to which the commitment to executive branch unity is less a question of principle than a belief that oversight or judicial review is a mere inconvenience when compared to the prospect of aggrandized presidential power.

Congress's choice to delegate oversight responsibilities may resolve otherwise incommensurable debates about the lines of delineation between ministerial versus political responsibilities. By delegating legislative monitoring powers to government officials or private citizens, Congress removes itself as a party in dispute with the executive branch. And such a removal permits the courts to set limitations on these monitoring agents without infringing upon congressional prerogatives. A Freedom of Information Act requestor cannot obtain records controlled by the president or the deliberative policy discussions of agency officials. An Inspector General is statutorily limited to examining mismanagement in programs and operations and is barred from subpoenaing records from department employees. The Comptroller General is limited to auditing

[26] *See e.g., Hannah v. Larche*, 363 U.S. 420, 440–441 (1960) ("As is apparent from this brief sketch of the statutory duties imposed upon the Commission, its function is purely investigative and fact-finding. It does not adjudicate. It does not hold trials or determine anyone's civil or criminal liability. It does not issue orders. Nor does it indict, punish, or impose any legal sanctions. It does not make determinations depriving anyone of his life, liberty, or property. In short, the Commission does not and cannot take any affirmative action which will affect an individual's legal rights. The only purpose of its existence is to find facts which may subsequently be used as the basis for legislative or executive action").

agency expenditures, not examining policy choices. The Federal Trade Commission may investigate businesses under its "unfair or deceptive acts or practices" authority granted by Congress but can only enforce penalties under the oversight of the Department of Justice. These forms of monitoring are not only limited to ministerial functions, but they are forms of oversight where Congress need not act directly.

When Congress chooses to delegate its oversight and depend upon information obtained by those agents, oversight is not only limited to information about ministerial responsibilities but oversight is also unable to reach those offices and officers whose function is to serve the president or where access to their information would impede a constitutional duty of the president. Under such circumstances, oversight is limited not just to "bureaucratic information" but to "bureaucratic offices" as well. When Congress does have an interest in obtaining information about constitutional responsibilities or directly superintend political officers, Congress has a readily available tool: impeachment. By strategically delegating its monitoring powers, Congress is able to efficiently allocate direct congressional attention to those matters most likely to bear political or electoral fruit. While such an interpretation may limit the scope of the presidential administration of the executive branch, it also limits the sorts of interbranch information disputes that can be resolved by the courts. As has been argued throughout this book, procedural oversight over the bureaucracy's legislative activities in the form of investigations, rules, and orders is directly enforced not by Congress but by its agents, whether companies and their trade associations securing a judicial remedy or the GAO and Inspectors General sharing investigative findings that inform legislative action by Congress (collectively "fire alarms"). In this sense, whether the administrative state can be conceived of as a tenuous coexistence between presidential departments of an executive character and legislative agencies not so unlike congressional committees, or is instead a unitary enforcement state subject to congressional and administrative oversight, rests upon the activities of the FOIA requesters, APA litigants and Inspectors General who have been empowered to set the oversight agenda.

But if administrative law is about the enforcement of legislative procedure through organized interests and agency investigations are considered one method, among others, bureaucrats choose for implementing public policy, then a number of important ramifications follow. First, the theory of the unitary executive as requiring the executive branch to speak in one voice, namely one controlled by the president, fails on grounds that the bureaucracy's investigative powers are constrained by legislative interests in policy, not executive interests in law enforcement.[27] In fact, if investigative powers of the bureaucracy are both delegated from Congress and subject to congressional monitoring, it dilutes the authority of the president if he is expected to supervise such policy implementation as part of his core constitutional enforcement powers. Second, as a legislative institution, we should question the president's role in supervising the bureaucracy at all. That is to say, while certain departments exercise core executive functions the agencies that implement delegated legislative authority, those so-called "quasi-legislative, quasi-judicial" agencies like the Federal Trade Commission (FTC) or the Merit Systems Protection Board (MSPB), should not be headed by presidential appointees but, instead, subject only to congressional supervision. In essence, there is no basis to distinguish the ministerial bureaucracy from a congressional committee.[28] On the other hand, for Congress to exercise control over presidentially controlled officials exercising constitutional discretion raises separation of powers issues. Third, if, as a matter of political theory, the administrative state as such is indistinguishable from the several committees of Congress, then the use of administrative procedures to punish or reward special interests should be navigated outside the judiciary and, therefore, disputes should be considered political, not legal, matters (this is already the case when special interest groups submit complaints to the Office of Special Counsel or Offices of Inspectors General).

4 Pluralistic, Not Unitary, Sovereignty

The expression, "the administrative state" is ubiquitous within political discussions today. Its recent popularity stems from a growing skepticism of centralized, regulatory control over the private sphere. Unlike the tensions between government and liberty common to the themes of America's own founding, this skepticism is grounded in a concern about abdication of power from one branch—the legislative—to another—the executive.

[27] Christine Kexel Chabot, *Interring the Unitary Executive*, 98 Notre Dame L. Rev. 129 (2022).

[28] *See* Buckley v. Valeo, *infra*.

What is perhaps odd about the chorus of voices critical of the growth of federal bureaucracy is their proposed solution. A crucial fix entails granting the President increased oversight over bureaucratic functions (and relying on the federal courts to reform policy therein). Concerned that the SEC's in-house judges are acting arbitrarily? Ensure they are appointed by the President. Bitter that the EPA writes rules outside the plain meaning of legislative text? Claim that all rulemaking is subject to the enforcement power of the President and therefore under his supervision. The thought is that unconstitutional delegations of legislative power to the bureaucracy can be reinterpreted (and justified) as constitutional authorizations of presidential power. For these lawyers, delegation of legislative power from Congress to the executive branch is impermissible under a strict interpretation of the separation of powers. This nondelegation doctrine applies to all attempts to assign legislative powers to the executive department. And, to be logically consistent, that includes legislative investigations, adjudications and rulemaking since legal doctrine justifies the former as auxiliaries to the latter. The doctrine requires any ceding of responsibility from the legislative branch to the executive be guided by intelligible, guiding legislative principles to prevent the now-empowered executive branch from inappropriately making policy. Without intelligible principles, ceding power in this way is not (impermissible) delegation at all—but lawful authorization of power. The difficulty, here, however, is that a major political-philosophical concern animating the Constitution is ensuring the federal executive power is minimized in scope. Whether the above is described as legislative abdication or executive aggrandizement, a larger executive branch is an inevitable result.

This book models the effects of delegation on oversight to defend a causal relationship between these two concepts. But this book also reorients the starting definitions of congressional politics through a historical and jurisprudential investigation. I defend the legislative power as broader than mere rulemaking but inclusive of powers to investigate and adjudicate with respect to the private sphere. Congressional investigations and adjudication are policymaking. And my argument is that Congress has shown it can delegate these less prominent legislative powers. My contention is that oversight is something distinguishable from Congress's investigative power writ large and meaningfully describes investigations unique to delegated legislative power. It is uncontroversial to say that the early Congress's inquiries of executive branch activity did not involve oversight of delegated authority. At the same time, it is uncontroversial to argue that the broad concept of congressional oversight is distinct from other constitutional bases for congressional investigations such as the impeachment power. Thus "oversight" in the sense of investigations, hearings, and floor activity aimed at the bureaucracy is distinct from the rulemaking activity in which ministerial duties or obligations are placed upon the executive branch through statute.

This new unitary theory affirms, in the abstract, principles of constitutional structure that ensure contestation between the branches. But as this book shows, subjecting the president to compulsory oversight by Congress has the effect of superintending the president to the political will of a coordinated branch. And the new unitarist solution, an aggressive form of unitary executive theory, also tends to overlook the nature of legislative power defended in this book. Legislative policymaking involves writing rules but it also involves investigations which serve an informing function. But when an executive branch can claim more investigative authority to advance its policy goals, it is foreseeable that such investigative powers will not be readily cabined within the procedures and process of legislative rulemaking but unencumbered in ways resembling the president's constitutional prerogative to enforce the law with discretion.

The controversy concerning the delegation of legislative powers to the modern federal bureaucracy is one of degree, not of kind. This book forces administrative law and policy debates to work off a scientific foundation of legislative power understood as something more than just the power to make rules. The historical examination of this book reveals that the administrative state arose not from a decision by Congress to empower agencies with rulemaking power but to empower these agencies to investigate the private sphere for the purpose of informing Congress about policy. In this sense, the administrative subpoena powers Congress authorized to the agencies mirrored Congress's own investigative powers over the private sphere. Over time, Congress delegated rulemaking and ratemaking authorities to the agencies so that agency investigations could be used to advance the policies written by the agencies rather than for Congress to be charged with such complex policymaking. To describe those nineteenth and twentieth-century congresses as authorizing the early Interstate Commerce Commission or Federal Trade Commission with administrative subpoena powers to enhance those agencies' law enforcement prerogatives is inconsistent both with political intent as evidenced in floor debates at the time as well as constitutional analysis as reflected in twentieth-century Supreme Court cases like *McGrain v. Daugherty*, *Endicott Johnson Corp. v. Perkins*, or *Oklahoma Press Publishing v. Walling*. The plain text of the laws delegating administrative subpoena authorities to the bureaucracy made clear their purpose was legislative, not executive.

Regulatory threats to business are commonly described in terms of rules that impose compliance burdens and costs. But the federal administrative state does not primarily regulate through rules. Agency investigations of businesses, administrative enforcement, and adjudications that lead to binding orders reflect the primary regulatory activities of the federal administrative state. Businesses, particularly those whose primary regulatory obligations are federal in nature, prefer regulation via rules because of the clarity and certainty rules provide. When proposed rules may threaten business interests, those companies can get involved in the rulemaking process or petition for new rules. Similar procedures are not available when agencies investigate and bring enforcement actions even though agencies assert that their consent decrees and administrative law orders establish a form of regulatory common law that binds market participants within an industry.

The jurisprudential trend today is to identify all agency action—whether occurring in cabinet departments or in independent agencies—as "executive" in nature. The difficulty with this move is that no advocate of this strong executive power theory would argue that executive enforcement of administrative subpoenas against the private sphere should be subject to the same constitutional procedures as, for instance, search warrants by the FBI. What distinguished early legislative delegation from contemporary interpretations is that congressional delegation in the nineteenth and twentieth centuries was made to agencies that were subsidiary to Congress, not the President. As such, these agencies lacked executive authority. Congress was not seeking to aggrandize executive agencies with legislative power. As a technical matter, these agencies did not raise constitutional problems for their original authority did not involve the sort of law enforcement power the executive department and its agencies exercise.

And in making the move to view the civil service bureaucracy as an executive, versus legislative, these unitarists magnify the scope of presidential power far beyond the original understanding of the Constitution.

Political scientists in the tradition of Neustadt know well that a president charged with too broad a scope of responsibility, as is the modern administrative president, becomes an effective clerk of the legislative will. The strong unitary theory of the administrative state not only bloats the power of Washington, D.C., but it also weakens the efficiency of the President by burdening him with too much supervisory responsibility. The irony is that the administrative president's executive discretion becomes reduced to ministerial responsibilities subject to congressional oversight and public rights litigation. This picture is hardly one of an energetic unitary executive.

This book carefully supports the distinction between congressional investigations of the private sphere for a rulemaking purpose and congressional investigations of the executive branch for a political purpose. It also uses constitutional principles to examine the institution of congressional oversight in the development of American law. While congressional requests for information from the executive branch occurred as early as the American founding, this was distinct from the much more recent use of judicially enforceable legislative subpoenas against the executive branch. In fact, the first instance of a congressional subpoena to the executive branch was in the 1970s. There is certainly no original understanding of compulsory legislative process against the executive branch outside of constitutionally enumerated powers like impeachment.

Legal culture, as a matter of black letter rules and institutional norms, distinguishes between advocacy before committees (as lobbying) and representation of clients before agencies (litigation in the form of enforcement defense or petitions for remedial action). The notion that administrative procedures are policy tools means that a legalistic view of administrative (legislative) procedures, with the presumption of judicial review, encourages both legislative abdication and executive branch immunity from constitutional process. That the legislative process is largely exempt from constitutional liability for unreasonable seizures, lack of due process, or excessive penalties that attach to law enforcement activities ought to apply to any delegation of that process.

The pluralistic nature of administrative power is the democratic solution to the legislative refusal to use political remedies when the executive branch fails to accede to congressional oversight demands. The Constitution empowers Congress with a host of political remedies (appropriations riders, arrests via the Sergeant of Arms, refusal to confirm presidential nominees, impeachment, etc.) yet nowhere enumerates a legislative right to judicial review. Opposition to administrative pluralism has had a woeful historical record. Nazism's most astute legal apologist, Carl Schmitt, tellingly discredited the legal empowerment of publicly interested groups as creating a "pluralist party-state" hostile to the authority of the national sovereign leader.[29] But Schmitt's polemic is instructive, for an administrative state whose policymaking is authorized under its power to enforce the law, and where Congress chooses the convenience of litigation over the responsibility of inherent contempt, effectively delegates back to the people the legislative task of contestation and deliberation necessary for advancing public policy. The enforcement state leads to the crumbling of sovereignty because political power is devolved to special litigating interests.

[29] Carl Schmitt, Guardian of the Constitution, 131 (1931); *accord*. Carl Schmitt, *State Ethics and the Pluralist State*, in Jacobson & Schlink, Weimar: A Jurisprudence of Crisis (1930) at 306 ("When constitutional lawyers speak of the "omnipotence" of the sovereign— the king or the parliament— their baroquely exaggerated formulas should be understood as owing to the fact that in the state of the sixteenth to eighteenth centuries the issue was overcoming the pluralist chaos of the churches and estates. One makes one's task too easy if one adheres to such idioms.... State unity was always a unity from social pluralities. At various times and in various countries it was very different but always complex and, in a certain sense, intrinsically pluralist. A reference to this self-evident complexity can perhaps refute an extravagant monism but does not solve the problem of political unity."). Schmitt viewed the legal empowerment of political groups as politicizing civil society institutions. *Id*. at 307 ("[a]mong pluralist theorists of the state as nearly everywhere, an error prevails that generally persists in uncritical unconsciousness— that the political signifies a specific substance, next to the substance of other 'social associations'; that it represents a specific content besides religion, economy, language, culture, and law; and that, therefore, the political group can be understood as standing coordinately next to the other groups— the church, combine, union, nation, cultural and legal communities of all sorts. Political unity thus becomes a special, new substantial unity, joining other unities. Any debates and discussions on the nature of the state and the political will become confused as long as the widespread idea prevails that a political sphere with its own content exists side by side with other spheres").

Index

D. Z. Epstein, *The Investigative State: Regulatory Oversight in the United States*, https://doi.org/10.1007/978-3-031-38461-5

Printed in the USA
CPSIA information can be obtained
at www.ICGtesting.com
LVHW051045310723
753868LV00009B/606

9 783031 384608